# EFFECTIVE JEWISH PARENTING

MIRIAM LEVI

# EFFECTIVE JEWISH PARENTING

 FELDHEIM PUBLISHERS

*New York / Jerusalem*

First published 1986 · ISBN 0-87306-405-4

Philipp Feldheim Inc.
200 Airport Executive Park
Spring Valley, NY 10977

Feldheim Publishers Ltd.
POB 6525 / Jerusalem, Israel
Printed in Israel

In memory of my dear father

HENRY E. WECHSLER ז״ל

who by his personal example
taught me the meaning of *chesed*.
He cared for those in need
and worked tirelessly to alleviate their lot.

\*

and in memory of our beloved son

MEIR ז״ל

Blessed with an unusually keen mind
he was taken from us in his seventh year
when he already displayed a boundless joy and enthusiasm
for Torah learning.

# Preface

by Rabbi Simon Schwab

פיה פתחה בחכמה ותורת־חסד על לשונה. (משלי ל״יא)

"She opens her mouth with wisdom and the law of loving-kindness is on her tongue."

This posuk describes adequately this beautiful book by Mrs. Miriam Levi. She has become a teacher of contemporary Jewish parents and all her lessons have one common denominator, namely תורת חסד. She draws from reliable Torah sources and her own pedagogical experience how to cope with most of the common problems of child rearing. The secret is the re-education of parents by introspection into their own emotional life. The mitzvohs of honor and respect for parents are clearly defined as well as the methods of teaching obedience to children.

This is a very fascinating and valuable book for which we have to be deeply grateful to the author.

# Foreword

by Rabbi Nachman Bulman

A generation ago, the challenge faced by parents and educators in the Torah community seemed centered on matters of faith and practice. The tide of that battle has turned spectacularly in our favor and not only within the observant community. Unknown thousands are today magnetically drawn to mitzvah-observance from utmost alienation.

In the sphere of character and values, today's challenge is all the more threatening, precisely because its roots are less easily perceived.

The thirteen principles of our faith are definable. The *halakhah* indicates which deeds are commanded and which prohibited.

Today's parents are not on equally safe ground when they encounter the will, emotion, and habit patterns of their children. They face obvious questions.

Are they models of Torah authority or bullying tyrants?

Is their childrearing a reflection of neurotic complexes or of Torah insights?

Conversely, when they rely on exclusive voluntarism based on "explaining it to Moisheleh or Saraleh," are they educating their children, or surrendering to the values of a secular society and its unbridled permissiveness? In which case, a new generation might grow to adulthood, whose mitzvah-behavior might seem exemplary, but whose ego, emotions, and habits (in the sphere of non-formal mitzvah-practice) might be wildly unresponsive to Torah judgment. Can we remain oblivious when much of the above is no longer mere apprehension, but painful reality?

To harmonize those extremes, a high order of parental self-knowledge is necessary, as well as the keenest of insight into the soul of the child and the dynamics of his growth.

Coupled with such understanding — in fact, preceding

it — a systematic exposition is vitally needed, of Torah perspectives on the function of emotion, instinct, and habit in
child and adult, and especially on how those soul and body
powers may be "educated" and refined.

There is a particular difficulty in the matter of bringing
Torah wisdom to bear on the issues at hand.

Classical Torah sources reflect different principles of
organization and exposition from those that are familiar to
most Jews in the west. The idiom of those sources, for all their
perfect applicability, makes Torah guidance not easily acces-
sible to all but deeply initiated students of Torah. On the other
hand, the pervasive message of secular educational theory all
but floods our consciousness. For many, the temptation to
distort Torah values, by "tailoring" seemingly "liberal" Torah
sources, becomes the more difficult to resist. Nor does a
protective authoritarianism insulate a minority of children
against being deeply affected by the wild permissiveness of
today's majority of children.

In either case the parent loses control, and the child may
be deprived of the noblest aspects of his heritage.

What alternative remains for those whose who believe that
a clear exposition of the teachings of Torah on raising children
would immeasurably enhance our role as parents; that such an
exposition would verify beyond dispute that our "authoritarianism" is the means to our children's true liberty, while our
"libertarianism" actually leads to their "enslavement"?

Miriam Levi has authored a major work on the subject for
which many will be grateful.

The fourteen chapters of *Effective Jewish Parenting* are a
wide-ranging digest of Torah teaching on the challenge of
contemporary upbringing of Jewish children. Her sources are
painstakingly researched and listed. Her seeming simplicity of
style is rooted in elemental clarity, not mediocrity. She does not
preach, but engages in a genuine teaching dialogue with her
unseen readers. Her theory does not remain suspended in
abstraction, but is always applied with a wealth of illustration.

Not the least achievement of the authoress is her judicious use of the theory of cognitive psychology, to convey in contemporary idiom much that illustrates Torah thought on respective issues — all in total faithfulness to Torah, without apologetics.

The parent is initially moved to introspection on his own emotional life, prior to consideration of how to instill the mitzvah of honoring parents.

He is then led to seek a balance between firmness of position and stimulating a child's self-motivation; between love, discipline, mutual understanding and consideration.

Training for orderly home behavior is next considered, and is followed by problems of emotional expression (jealousy, fighting, crying).

The cultivation of a supportive relation to the child's schooling is explored, and the work closes with suggestions on six widespread problems that parents face from time to time.

It is the hope of the writer of these lines, that *Effective Jewish Parenting* will come to be recognized as a wonderful means for the most precious of goals: rearing the coming generation of the People of the Torah.

On the way to that noblest of achievements, not a few parents may discover that they are reeducating themselves as well; that the proverbial, elusive hope, "if we could only relive some of our childhood" need not be an epitaph of despair, but a prod to heroic striving. "And he shall restore the heart of the fathers *through* (Rashi) the children." (Rashi, Malakhi 3:24)

If in the process of raising our children we feel impelled to *teshuvah* in deed, in character, and in soul, can there be a more striking indication that our final redemption is near?

# Acknowledgments

My boundless thanks to my husband Leo, who established the Torah foundation of this book, unstintingly provided invaluable counseling and editing help, and composed the notes at the end of the volume. He has made a major contribution without which, in fact, the book could not have been written at all but would have remained an idea in the mind of its author.

Special thanks are due to my sons Yoseph, Shlomoh, and Hillel for their useful contributions and for their patience while mother was working on "the book."

My heartfelt appreciation goes to David Hornik for his expert editing.

I want to thank Miriam Adahan for reviewing Chapter 1 and making many helpful suggestions.

I am grateful also to the mothers who read some of the material and offered their reactions.

Lastly, I thank the parents who shared with me their experiences and contributed their stories, which have so enriched this book.

M. L.

# CONTENTS

# Contents

# Contents

# Introduction

Parents have been raising and educating children for thousands of years, but never has there been so much interest in this subject as in our time. Hundreds of authoritative books on child care have been written, yet parents seem to be having more difficulties with their children than ever before. Disciplinary problems in particular are on the rise, and many parents are at a loss as to what to do about it.

In previous generations, mothers and fathers largely followed the example of their parents. Traditional practices went unchallenged. Parents were clearly in a position of authority. Children were aware of their duties. Our generation, however, has rejected many of the structures of the past, including most of the time-honored childrearing methods. New principles of childrearing, based on the idea of complete equality between parents and children, have been formulated. There are experts who theorize that children can no longer be expected to obey their parents, but must be encouraged into voluntary cooperation. Moreover, psychologists have alarmed everyone about the dire effects of inept parenting on the vulnerable psyches of young children.

Thus stripped of their authority, parents have become increasingly uncertain and confused. Whereas once parents trusted their capacity to raise children, many now self-consciously re-examine their decisions, their actions, and their conversations, for parental misdemeanors which could implant insecurities and neurotic complexes in their children. For these parents, childrearing has become a tense, guilt-ridden ordeal rather than the satisfying and creative experience it was meant to be.

Fortunately, Jewish parents who have Torah as their guide still accept that parenthood is a position of authority and control. Judaism cannot accept any relinquishment of parental responsibility. Torah teaches parents to see their children as a divine trust.[1] Their task, to educate their child to a life of service to God, is a sacred one.[2] Primarily, it requires the parents to set for the child a lofty example of those character traits they wish to develop in him. But this alone is not enough. There will always be occasions when, to provide the necessary guidance, parents must assert their authority. Furthermore, the mitzvah of honoring and revering parents precludes any egalitarian relationship. While Torah does see parents and children as equal in value, it assigns them different roles and responsibilities.

Still, many Jewish parents have to some extent been influenced by our times, and are confused and uncertain about their role. Moreover, while it was never an easy task to raise children, today's affluence and moral decay have made the job more difficult than ever before. Thus, many Jewish parents need clear guidance on childrearing problems, based on Torah teachings.

Modern guidance books for parents have criticized the "old" methods of childrearing as harsh, oppressive, and insensitive. Yet if we examine the Torah approach to child discipline, we will find, quite to the contrary, that it is warm and loving, and grants the child great freedom within certain limits. The Gaon of Vilna, famed Torah sage of the eighteenth century, wrote that children should be admonished with "soft words and reprimands which will be willingly accepted."[3] The noted educator, Rabbi Samson Raphael Hirsch writes, "Never request a child to do something unnecessary and unimportant; similarly don't refuse a harmless and trivial request. . . . Let your child do and have whatever you can permit him, on the condition that it won't endanger his physical and moral well-being."[4]

Guidance on practical issues, however, is ineffective if parents have not learned the emotional control necessary to put Torah values into practice. It is not enough merely to tell parents to reprimand calmly and not get angry — they usually know that. They need to learn *how* to accomplish this. While the Torah contains specific advice on the problems of child-rearing, many people seem to have difficulty applying that advice in practice.

What is needed is a method of coping with emotions which reasserts Torah perspectives. Cognitive psychology, a recently developed system, answers this need. It teaches that we have the ability to change our basic outlook and behavior, and puts control into the hands of the individual.

Cognitive psychology teaches that it is not the events in our lives themselves that disturb us, but the way we have learned to interpret and evaluate them. This approach aims to change our basic, problem-causing beliefs, enabling us to see our life's events in a more positive light. As a result, we function better and increase the satisfaction in our lives.

In the childrearing situation, parents who wish to change the way they react to their child must learn first to *think* differently about the child's behavior. The natural result is that parents will then *feel* differently about that behavior. They will then be in better control of their own behavior and find it easier to alter it.

Once we have begun to change our characteristic way of reacting to situations, we find that this in turn changes our feelings and way of thinking. Our sages have taught: "A man is shaped by his actions; his heart and all his thoughts always [follow after] his activities."[5] When we work to change our customary behavior, we also establish new, more positive patterns of thinking and feeling. These, in turn, reinforce our new habits of behavior. Essentially, we reverse the vicious cycle wherein children misbehave, parents become upset and react non-constructively, and the misbehavior continues.

In this book, we will draw on the educational teachings of Torah authorities throughout the generations. And we will use modern cognitive psychological findings as a tool for putting into practice the teachings of our sages.

# EFFECTIVE JEWISH PARENTING

# The Foundation: Learning to Cope With Our Emotions

In managing their children, the most difficult part for parents is coping with their own emotions. "What can I do?" says one mother; "I know I shouldn't get angry, but my kids get me so mad when they fight that before I know it, I'm yelling and screaming at them." Another mother reports, "After I've lost my temper at my kids I feel so guilty. Then I try to make it up to them by being overly permissive."

These parents realize that, by allowing their feelings to get in the way, they react to their children inappropriately. If we want to be more effective parents, we must find a way to cope with our emotions. Otherwise, we will be locked in an exhausting and never-ending struggle to keep them under control. Under such conditions, we will have great difficulty achieving our educational goals.

Where do these overpowering emotions come from? People often say, "*That* made me so mad!" or "*He* made me feel so guilty!" as if outside events produce our emotions. Yet according to the modern cognitive approach,[1] we bring on emotions ourselves, with the *interpretations* we give to events. In other words, our emotions are not imposed on us. They result largely from the things we tell ourselves, from our thoughts. Thus, we feel the way we think.

1

According to this theory, our thinking takes the form of little inner conversations with ourselves. While we are sometimes aware of these "inner dialogues," at other times they occur so swiftly and subtly that we don't sense them at all. Yet we know only too well the feelings and behaviors which result from these dialogues. With practice, we can learn to identify these upsetting thoughts which set off our emotions. We can challenge the beliefs on which they are based, and gradually change them. This will create a calmer and more relaxed emotional state. By learning to control and prevent emotions which cause self-defeating behavior, we can even alter long established habits. Once we have brought our emotions under control, we will be much better able to handle the problems of childrearing.

In this chapter we will focus on two of the most troublesome emotions that parents encounter in dealing with children: anger and guilt.

## What Makes Us Angry?

Anger is the major problem for parents and is one of the most destructive forces within the family. "Anger in the home," states the Talmud, "is like worms in grain," bringing total dissolution.[2] "All kinds of hell rule over the person who is constantly angry";[3] "His life is no life."[4] Most quick-tempered people are aware of the harmful effects of their anger, and of the misery it causes them. However, they are generally helpless to do much about it, because they are unaware of the underlying causes of their anger.

The thought process beneath anger is usually the expectation that life should always go the way we want it to. The Talmud speaks of anger as a "false god within you."[5] This "god" decrees how everything must be. When people or situations contradict this decree, the person breaks out in angry condemnations. Perhaps this is what the Sages referred to when they said, "He who gets angry, is as if he worships idols."[6]

Our demand that everything must be as *we* want, underlies our anger toward our children as well. For example, mothers frequently get angry and scream at their children for leaving a messy room. However, it is not disorder in her children's room which creates a mother's anger, but what she tells herself about it. If she thought, "What a mess! I wish the kids wouldn't leave their room like this," her emotional reaction would be mild. She would feel unhappy, but probably not unduly disturbed. However, an angry mother is more likely to be telling herself, "Never in my life have I seen such a horrible mess! Why are my kids such dreadful slobs! Why *can't* they keep their room in order!" Implied in these complaints is a *demand*: "My children *must* keep their room in order!" We may not always be aware of the demand, but it is there nevertheless.

But what, one might ask, is wrong with that? After all, orderliness is important and all parents should try to teach it to their children. The trouble is that when we are angry, our own demands for perfection are at the center of our message. What we are really saying is, "My children should always behave as *I* want!" This demand is unrealistic and irrational. The intention to train our children in orderliness is praiseworthy, but the angry way we do this interferes with our goal of fostering good character traits in them.

## INTOLERANCE

While such demands underlie most anger, they are not the *direct* cause of it. What initially triggers our anger is our assessment of how intolerable the situation is. When we are angry, we don't just think it's inconvenient that our children do not behave as we want them to. We tell ourselves that it's "terrible" and that we "can't stand it." When we insist that our children come immediately when called, regarding it as intolerable when they don't, or if we demand that they help out willingly and with pleasure, viewing it as unbearable when they grumble and make a fuss, we inevitably become angry. A mother who, when her children quarrel, thinks "They shouldn't fight so much" yet accepts the fighting as merely an unpleasant but normal aspect of sibling relations, will not be as upset as one who views it as "awful" and "unbearable."*

## NEGATIVE JUDGING

However, anger consists of more than intolerance of the situation. It also entails a judgment. When our children misbehave, we jump quickly from "I can't stand it!" to "They're bad kids!" For example, if we are furious with a child for not coming when called, we are not only upset about the "terrible" inconvenience we are being subjected to. We also blame and condemn the child, for causing our inconvenience. We are probably thinking to ourselves, "He heard me; he knew he should come; why didn't he? Obviously, he doesn't want to listen. He's just a bad child!" By ascribing bad motives to the child, we see *him* as bad. Our anger intensifies if we believe that the child misbehaves on purpose just to make us angry, or that he could behave better if he really wanted to.

We are not always aware of this negative judgment behind our anger. But when we remember the thoughts which accompanied our anger, we can readily discover it. For example, we might think to ourselves, when our child speaks

---

*The words should not be confused for the judgment they represent. It isn't the words in themselves that reveal our true view and determine our subsequent feelings. For example, we use the words "awful" and "terrible" when what we really mean is that the situation is merely unpleasant. "I can't stand their fighting," expressed with a sigh, does not necessarily indicate intolerance. But when we furiously declare, "I can't *stand* their fighting!" anyone can tell that we really mean it. Thus we might say, "I *don't like* the way this room looks!" indicating great intolerance. The same words, given a different tone, could mean quite another thing. Thus the way we express ourselves reveals our true feelings, much more than which words we use.

to us disrespectfully, "How dare he talk to me this way!" While there is no explicit negative evaluation of the child here, it is strongly implied. To reveal it, we only have to ask ourselves, "What is he for daring to talk to me this way? (a bad kid!)." Similarly, if we think, "He *shouldn't* talk to me this way!" we can continue our trend of thought, "and because he does, he is ... (a miserable child!)." We may not like to admit it, but the judgment is nearly always there.

Annoyance conveys the same negative judgments as does anger, but in a milder form. The evaluations are identical, but not nearly as extreme. On a scale of 0 to 10, we might put anger at a point between 6 and 10, depending on the intensity, whereas annoyance would be assigned a 1 or 2 if it is very mild, or 3 to 5 if it is stronger.

When we are annoyed, we tend to speak in a sharp tone of voice. We'll tell a child who is bothering his brother or sister, "Leave him alone!" or snap at a youngster who has ignored a request to remove the dishes from the table, "I thought I told you to clear the table!" Some parents resort to sarcasm when they are annoyed. They will remark to a child playing with his cup at the table, "I see you won't be satisfied until that breaks."

Because the negative judgments in annoyance are milder than in anger, we are apt to have greater difficulty identifying them.

## LOW FRUSTRATION TOLERANCE (LFT)

Parents who find themselves frequently getting angry at their children are probably suffering from low frustration tolerance (LFT). LFT is the belief that we cannot endure pain, discomfort, or frustration. Parents with LFT demand that their life must always be easy and comfortable; that they should not have to undergo suffering or inconvenience. Children, however, cause us no end of inconvenience as they grow up. They deprive us of sleep; they tie us down to the house; they cause us extra work; they are a financial burden; and, because they

5

have minds of their own, they do not always act exactly as we want them to.

Yet even though we might sometimes wish things to be different, we can nevertheless remain reasonably happy so long as we learn to accept these inconveniences and frustrations with equanimity. If we think to ourselves, however, as we clean up a child's milk mess on the floor, "Now I have this *terrible* mess to clean up. It's awful! I *shouldn't* have to work so hard!" we will invariably get angry over the situation — and also at the child who caused all the extra and disagreeable work.

Thus, our demand that annoying and frustrating situations *should not* exist, creates our wrath. We keep insisting that things must be different from the way they are, meaning, "Things should be the way *I* want, and I can't *stand* it when they aren't!" Annoyance or inconvenience in themselves cannot make us angry unless we tell ourselves, "I shouldn't be inconvenienced in this dreadful way!"

Observe the basic demand underlying anger: "I must have what I want!" When we do not get what we want, we are frustrated. The anger-producing thought is, "I can't *stand* the frustration of not having what I want!" Thus we get angry when we insist that we have quiet, yet have unbearable noise; or when we demand that our children be well-mannered and obedient, yet they are rude and unruly.

## Anger Doesn't Get Us Anywhere

If anger were an effective way of making children change their poor behavior, we would have seen an end to their misconduct long ago. Quite to the contrary, anger is one of the most ineffective ways to deal with children's misbehavior.

Suppose your five-year-old son regularly teases and hits his younger sister, making her cry. You have asked him to stop many times, yet he persists. Finally you lose patience and tell him angrily, "What's the matter with you? Why are you so mean to your little sister! Why can't you treat her nicely!" Your five-year-old is now even less motivated to change the way he treats his sister. If he accepts your negative evaluation, he will become preoccupied with thinking about how bad he is. If he rejects it, he will attempt to defend himself. Moreover, your attack is likely to make him feel resentful and rebellious toward you — hardly the best mood for compliance.

Thus anger defeats our goals.

In fact, our anger often reinforces the very behavior we wish to eliminate. In the child's eyes, our anger implies that he is bad. He then accepts this evaluation for himself, concluding, "This is the way I am. I guess I'll always act this way." So he continues in his negative behavior pattern.

Anger can, of course, frighten children into obeying, but this is accomplished at great cost to our relationship with them. Moreover, the results we obtain are temporary at best. In all likelihood, we will find ourselves resorting to anger continually to make our children comply. Eventually we will reach a point where we are forced to admit, "The only time they listen is when I get angry."

The well-known Torah scholar, Rabbi Simcha Wasserman, points out, "Parents should make up their minds what they want. If they want to vent anger, let them do so. But if they want to achieve something, they cannot do it by venting anger."[7]

Can controlling anger be harmful? While our sages have always denounced short-temperedness as a destructive character trait, modern psychology has taught that suppressing anger is harmful and has encouraged people to vent their anger instead. Some psychologists now challenge this ventilationist view of anger. Dr. Carol Tavris writes, "It seems to me that the major effect of the ventilationist approach has been to raise the general noise level of our lives, not to lessen our problems. I notice that the people who are most prone to give vent to their rage get angrier, not less angry."[8]

In the cognitive approach, however, anger is not held in

but is prevented in the first place by dealing with its root cause — our negative judgments and evaluations. Notice the difference between the two approaches in this mother's account:

> My son would not dress himself even though he was completely capable of doing it. Whenever I told him to dress himself, he would either ignore me or tell me I should do it. As I kept repeating myself, I found my tone of voice was getting more and more stern. I kept telling myself, "No, I will not lose control — I will not yell at him — I will not spank him." But with each time I had to repeat my request, I was getting more and more angry inside. Thinking over the situation later, I wondered where I was going wrong. I suddenly realized that the idea is not to remain in control while angry, but rather to remove the reasons for the anger in the first place. What helps me most is telling myself, "I am not going to achieve my goal through anger!" Now my son is starting to get dressed on his own, without being told. He doesn't do it all the time, but those few times are certainly a beginning. It proves to me that you can accomplish so much more when you are calm.

Some parents get angry at their child when they try to force him to obey their requests, justifying this on the basis of the child's Torah obligation to honor them. Yet, while children are indeed obliged to obey their parents,[9] we cannot *force* them to do so with any great success.

We must also keep in mind that Torah forbids us to act in a way that causes anguish to others.[10] Parents may not let out pent-up resentment toward the child for failing to meet their demands, because they thereby cause him unnecessary anguish. In fact, the child may well come to resent his parents for it.

Under special circumstances, parents may deliberately

act angry toward their child in order to correct improper behavior, even though it causes him anguish.[11] Such intentional anger is far different from the uncontrolled indignation which stems from not having our perfectionistic demands met. This deliberate anger must be reserved for those rare occasions when it is necessary to forcefully impress a child with the gravity of his wrongdoing.[12] However, one must remove all traces of anger from one's heart before one can effectively use this mode of reprimand.

## Getting Rid of Anger

### CONCERN FOR THE CHILD'S WELFARE

The first step in preventing anger is to give up our demands for perfection and convenience. We must begin to focus not on what *we* want but on the child's welfare. For example, if we want to avoid getting angry at our children over their messy room, we should stop focusing on our personal displeasure. Instead, we should think how orderliness helps our children function more effectively. From there we can start looking for constructive solutions to the problem of the messy room.

### LEARNING TO COPE WITH FRUSTRATION

Remember, the anger we experience when we are inconvenienced or frustrated stems not from the inconveniencing or frustrating situation itself, but rather from our evaluation of it as unbearable. While a child's continuous whining and crying is irritating, it makes us angry only because we tell ourselves that we can't *stand* the irritation. The underlying cause of our anger is our *demand* for a trouble-free and comfortable life. When we are angry over the crying, we do not tell ourselves that we *prefer* not being disturbed by the noise, viewing it merely as a tolerable nuisance. Rather, we tell ourselves that we *should not* be disturbed in this awful way, that it is intolerable, and we can't stand it for another minute!

9

It is the escalation of a *preference* for a life free of trouble and frustration into a *demand* for it which leads to our anger. Therefore the first step in eliminating the anger is to give up this demand, to stop insisting that because we prefer such an easy existence, we *must* have it. It is, after all, a little foolish to expect that anyone could ever lead a trouble-free life!

Giving up this demand is not easy. It is especially hard when we have been accustomed for years to believing that if we want something, we *must* have it. We need to be tough with ourselves and challenge this basic belief. After all, just because we would like the children to get along well, *must* it therefore be that way? Because we would prefer never to undergo inconvenience or frustration, does it then *have* to be like that?

It is pointless to tell ourselves, when something doesn't go our way, that we simply can't stand it. After all, we continue to exist. This is obvious proof that we can very well stand it, even though we may never exactly like it.

Imagine someone at the window on a rainy day, looking out on the downpour and angrily declaring, "It shouldn't be raining; the sun must come out!" When you find yourself becoming angry and thinking, "Things shouldn't be this way!" is what you are doing any different? Life will frequently be difficult and frustrating; we might as well accept this fact and learn to live with it.

You are tired and exhausted because a sick child kept you up all night, and you are worried about how you will manage to get your work done the next day. Don't make yourself angry by thinking, "It shouldn't be this way; I shouldn't have such a difficult life!" Tell yourself, instead, "I've had a rough night. I'll be tired and probably find it difficult to get my work done, but I guess I can cope." The next time your children fight, don't become enraged by telling yourself, "They shouldn't be this way; they shouldn't cause me so much aggravation!" Tell yourself, rather, "It's a shame that they're acting like this, but let me see what I can do about the situation."

The essence is to avoid extreme or exaggerated appraisals. A child has been crying for over an hour. It seems natural to cry out, "I can't *stand* this horrible crying for another minute!" But it is more adaptive to substitute a more modest complaint. "His crying gets on my nerves, but it's not unbearable. I can live through it." We can think to ourselves, as we clean up the spilled milk, "I don't like doing this, but it's not so awful." Telling ourselves that we shouldn't have the horrible mess to clean up is what makes the job so very disagreeable. We can learn to adopt a more tolerant and accepting attitude toward life's difficulties.

It is helpful, too, to keep in mind that we only add to our problems by getting upset over them. We might dislike mopping up the spilled milk. But when we get angry because we have extra work, then we have, in addition to the work, our upset feelings to contend with. Thus we cause ourselves much additional and unnecessary suffering.

When we can accept whatever frustration and difficulties come our way, we will have eliminated a major cause of much needless anger and aggravation. We will also find ourselves far better able to cope effectively with troublesome situations when they arise.

## JUDGING FAVORABLY

The other major source of needless anger toward our children is our habit of judging and condemning them for their deficiencies. If we want to avoid getting angry, we must learn to judge our children favorably, despite their obvious shortcomings.

In general, Judaism opposes negative judgments and evaluations of others. The Sages teach, "Don't judge your fellow man until you are in his place."[13] The Meiri comments, "If you see someone transgress ... don't judge him unfavorably ... it is sometimes very difficult to resist temptation. If you had been similarly tempted, perhaps you would not have exercised

[more] self-control." Since we can never put ourselves exactly in someone else's position, it follows that we really cannot judge anyone. Our children are no exception. We must accept that judgment is God's domain alone, for only He can rate a person's merits against his sins.[14]

We should not only refrain from negative judgment, we are also taught to judge our fellow man favorably and give him the benefit of the doubt whenever possible.[15] Rabbi Samson Raphael Hirsch writes:

> Even if you see him sin with your own eyes, or if credible witnesses testify to his guilt — you are not the judge; for you, justice in this case means love; and in this love he finds his most trusty advocate, who excuses his act wherever possible, or at least looks for mitigating circumstances.[16]

We should, whenever possible, give our child the benefit of the doubt. The child who did not come when called may simply not have heard us. If it is clear, however, that the child heard us and is aware of his disobedience, we should speak to him about it without any suspicion that he deliberately intended to do wrong. Just because the child behaved incorrectly, you do not have to evaluate him negatively. Instead, you should look for extenuating circumstances for his behavior (e.g., he just didn't want to leave his friend). This does not excuse the behavior. The child should be quietly but firmly told, "I know it's hard to leave your friend while you're playing, but when I call you, you must come." Parents should not hesitate to assert themselves, but they should do it without making negative judgments.

It is especially easy to judge a child unfavorably for continued misbehavior despite repeated reprimands. Parents tell themselves, "He could behave differently if he really wanted to!" They would do well to remember that change is difficult and takes time and effort. Rabbi Simcha Zissel Ziv once told the spiritual director of his yeshiva that very often a teacher will become angry with a student who is rebuked three or four times and still does not obey. Before losing patience, suggests Rabbi Simcha Zissel, the teacher should ask himself if he always corrects his own shortcomings by the third or fourth reminder.[17]

One of the most frequent negative judgments parents make when confronted with a misbehaving child is that he misbehaves only in order to annoy them. They must, however, assume that there are some mitigating circumstances, even if it appears that the child misbehaves on purpose. For instance, instead of viewing the child's teasing of his younger sister as a deliberate attempt to be irritating, a favorable interpretation of his action might be: "He's not trying to annoy me; he does this because he's used to it." Similarly, instead of getting angry when our child shouts at us for not granting him some wish, we can tell ourselves, "I know he doesn't intend to hurt me. It's just that he hasn't yet learned to tolerate being frustrated. He hasn't yet developed self-control."

It helps check our anger, too, if we keep in mind that the child may sincerely regret his poor behavior and feel remorse over it afterwards.

## DISTINGUISHING BETWEEN THE CHILD AND HIS BEHAVIOR

To avoid getting angry at your child, don't think he himself is bad when he misbehaves. While his *behavior* may be poor, we should not judge *him* poorly because of it. We must learn to distinguish between the deed and the doer. For instance, your child may argue with you about washing the dishes. If you think to yourself, "He always argues when I tell him to do something! He's so inconsiderate and spoiled!" you are bound to criticize him angrily. Instead, separate the child from his behavior by telling yourself, "He has a bad habit of arguing when asked to do something." You are then more likely to find yourself feeling calm, and in a much better position to handle the situation constructively. (For example, you can simply avoid responding to the child's arguments, and pleasantly but firmly repeat your request about doing the dishes.) Keep in mind: It's not him, it's his bad habit. *The child does not equal his behavior.*

## STRESS

Guarding against exaggerations and negative judgments can prevent angry reactions, but there are often circumstances which increase our emotional sensitivity. It is harder to cope with frustration when we are under nervous or physical strain, or just having an especially hard day. We should keep in mind that pain, illness, trying experiences, lack of sleep, and fatigue are all likely to lower both our resistance and our frustration tolerance. We must expect to have a harder time controlling anger under such circumstances. But we must also learn to accept this, and to try to maintain some inner calm by recognizing that there are techniques we can use during trying times. Remember also to give yourself a well-earned pat on the back whenever you *do* succeed in controlling yourself while under stress.

A lot of our stress, however, comes from pressure we put on ourselves. We all know that it is harder to stay calm when we are trying to meet many demands. This is why it is so important for parents to set their priorities in order. We are far more likely to snap angrily at our children when we are trying to get a whole lot of things done in a hurry. Parents need to ask themselves such questions as, "What is more important, a spic-and-span house or a warm and easy relationship with my children?" "Must I really slave to prepare a host of special dishes for an elaborate Shabbath menu, or wouldn't it be better to settle for a simpler menu and buy cake at the bakery, as long as my children are all still little?"

Keeping our priorities in order in this way requires a

certain amount of inner strength. We cannot allow ourselves to worry about what visitors might think of us because our house isn't quite as clean as they think it should be, or because we haven't served them home-baked cake.

Then there is a kind of parental outburst which tends to follow a series of minor "disasters." It is typically brought on by the following thoughts: "This is just too much. I've held on to myself long enough now. I can't take it anymore." Underlying these thoughts we often find the following reasoning: "How long can I be expected to control myself and remain calm?" The assumption is that it is unreasonable for anyone to expect of us that we stay calm under such circumstances, and with one more "disaster" we'll have the right to explode.

When parents become aware of these thoughts, they can attempt to challenge their validity. It becomes increasingly difficult and requires greater effort to remain in control with each successive mishap, but it can be done.

When parents feel they are on the verge of screaming, they should control the urge and instead give quiet expression to their feelings. Telling the children, "Kids, this is a little too much for me" does no harm; it is the screaming which we should try our best to avoid.

While every effort should be made to prevent anger, it is neither possible nor desirable to remain *completely* calm at all times. It is appropriate and beneficial for the child to see sometimes that a particular action of his has upset us. A well-placed comment can often create sincerely felt regret. For instance, if two children who are involved in an argument begin to insult each other, we can say — but quietly — "It upsets me very much to see you kids being mean to one another." When we have left a clean and tidy kitchen, and come back half an hour later to find it in total disarray, we can let the child who left the mess know how much it distresses us. The thing to avoid is not emotional reaction, but raised voices and character judgments.

Finally, there is a special frustration that develops out of the learning process. Parents who have worked hard and have made good progress learning to control their anger, are likely to feel intensely disappointed and frustrated whenever they slide back into old habits. Regressions, however, are a normal part of the improvement process. They will inevitably occur sooner or later. But each time we do regress, we will become more aware of the dysfunctional beliefs which underlie our anger. That awareness will produce ever greater growth and change.

## ACCEPTING OUR LOT

By using the approach outlined in this book, we may reduce and even eliminate our anger. There is yet a higher level of coping with frustration; a serene acceptance of what life brings us. Acceptance is the secure feeling that we are in God's hands. We trust that whatever He decrees as our fate is for the good. Achieving this lofty level of trust (*bitachon*) is a lifetime endeavor. All we can do is strive continuously to come closer to it. We do not have to despair if we as yet lack this quality, for we can work to develop and strengthen it.

In short, we should make reasonable efforts to improve our lives, changing those things which can be changed. Trust in God enables us to accept with serenity that which cannot be changed. Armed with *bitachon*, we will have the courage and strength to endure whatever frustration or suffering befalls us. We know that God directs the whole world for the good. Perhaps we are being tested. Perhaps suffering is intended to develop in us new character traits, new strengths or insights. The good in our suffering is often not evident to our short-sighted view; we cannot expect to comprehend God's plan. But we must try to accept it without question. Thus we come to accept our portion in life, whatever it may be, ultimately achieving what we so much wish for — true inner peace.

# Guilt

Some of us are trying to be perfect. We see any imperfections on our part as signs of failure, and a proof of our worthlessness. Frequently we are as critical of ourselves as we are of our children, showing no more tolerance toward our own short-comings than toward theirs. Our habit of self-criticism may be so ingrained that we are, literally, at it all day, subjecting ourselves to a continuous harangue of accusation and abuse, ending up feeling spent and miserable. "Why am I always yelling at my children?" "I shouldn't be so demanding!" "Why can't I be more patient and reasonable?" "Why am I so easily frustrated?" "Why do I get annoyed so quickly?" "I shouldn't be so critical!" "I should give my children more attention." It is as if we harbor within us a critic who will not be stilled. He stands by, waiting to catch us at some wrongdoing or error, ready to pounce on us at any moment: "Look how bad you are!" "You did something wrong!" "You made a mistake!" "You shouldn't have done it!" "You'll never change!"

When parents become aware of the harmful effects of their anger and other failings, their anguish and remorse often only worsen. They ask themselves, "Why do I continue in this destructive pattern? Why do I spoil my relations with my children in this way?"

The wisest of all men said, "There is no righteous man on earth that does good and never sins."[18] No one can achieve perfection. Yet many of us insist that, as parents, we must never make mistakes or do anything wrong.

It is interesting that nowhere in the Torah do we find a requirement for perfection. Indeed, our sages taught us precisely the opposite. "It is not your obligation to complete the work, yet neither are you free to leave it."[19] While we are required to invest the necessary effort to fulfill our obligations, succeeding is not a requirement. When we condemn our children because they are not the perfect beings we demand them to be, we become angry. When we condemn ourselves because *we* are not the perfect parents we insist we must be, we feel guilty. Thus, guilt is anger turned inward. We are stricken with excessive remorse and anguish over our faulty behavior.

## *TESHUVAH:* THE TORAH METHOD OF DEALING WITH IMPERFECTION

Regret and remorse do have their place in our lives. They are healthy and constructive if they 1) arise from actual wrongdoing, and 2) lead to a resolve to avoid repetition of the faulty deed. This constitutes *teshuvah*, the Torah mechanism for behavior correction.

Rabbi Wasserman has compared *teshuvah* to a cleaning establishment: "If there were no cleaners, I would wear my suit until it became soiled, and then I would have to throw it out." Self-condemnation is like throwing out the suit; *teshuvah* takes out the spots.

Many people think we are required to repent only for active transgressions such as stealing. This is a mistake, says Rambam. We have to do *teshuvah* for anger, jealousy, and other bad character traits as well. And these, once they have become ingrained, are far more difficult to eradicate.[20]

The implementation of *teshuvah* depends on the ability to make choices.[21] This concept of a God-given *bechirah* (free will) is basic to Judaism. However, many people subscribe to the principle of *bechirah* in theory only, considering themselves incapable of it in practice. They believe that past hereditary or environmental influences make change virtually impossible. There is no denying the crucial role of such influences in shaping our past behavior. However, according to the cognitive view, they continue to affect our behavior today only because we keep reindoctrinating ourselves with the very same beliefs and thought patterns which formed our behavior originally. These beliefs and thought patterns are often highly irrational. They were developed during our childhood from our *interpretations* of the events in our lives at that time. Today, however, we can adopt new and more rational interpretations. This way we can release ourselves from the influences of the past.

This, to be sure, is not easy. Our thoughts, "inner dialogues," are usually rapid and automatic. Effort and practice are required merely to become aware of them and identify them. While we may consistently work hard to alter our way of thinking, habitual patterns will often take over, undermining our best efforts. Because of these difficulties, we are unlikely to succeed in completely eradicating the influences of the past. While in principle we are in control of our behavior and can change it freely at all times, in practice this freedom is often limited.

In an article on *teshuvah*, the late Rabbi Yechiel M. Schlessinger describes the proper sequence for correcting ingrained negative character traits. The reason we have such difficulty doing *teshuvah* for them, he explains, is that we go about it the wrong way. In *teshuvah* for a single act of wrongdoing, regret precedes correction. In changing long established habits, however, correction precedes regret. This is the order described by the prophet — "After I return, I regret"[22] — and outlined in the writings of both Rambam and Rabbenu Yonah. If one does *teshuvah* in the wrong order, he can become so engulfed in pain and sorrow over his behavior that he concludes that change is impossible.[23] In other words, when a person has a long-standing bad habit, he will never believe that he is actually capable of change until he sees himself improve.

The founder of the Mussar movement, Rabbi Yisrael of Salant, describes the road to character change as long, difficult, and full of obstacles. He is well known for saying, "It is easier to review the entire Talmud than to correct one trait." He teaches that it is important to realize that progress is inevitably followed by setbacks. Personality improvement is by nature slow. If we try to *force* change with our will, we can easily end up discouraged and even discontinue our effort.[24]

## SELF-DENIGRATION PREVENTS CHANGE

When we recognize that we have displayed poor character traits, we must do *teshuvah*. However, this does not call for endless regret or vicious attacks on ourselves. The Mishnah teaches, "Don't see yourself as wicked."[25] *Teshuvah*, properly executed, can allow for healthy and beneficial guilt, but it has no place for harmful and non-constructive guilt.

Underlying self-condemnation is a belief that because we have done something wrong, we must suffer for it. Such self-imposed suffering serves no useful purpose whatsoever. Indeed, self-denigration is often a major factor in perpetuating the very behavior we wish to change. Rambam comments on the Mishnah quoted above that if one has a low self-image, one learns to expect less of oneself and is bound to behave in a manner that meets these low expectations.[26]

Moreover, *teshuvah* demands a fairly high level of energy. Castigating ourselves diverts our energy into non-constructive channels, making change all the more difficult. As Rabbenu Yonah points out, a poor self-image leads to hopelessness, and is a major obstacle to proper repentance.[27] Therefore, any attempts to improve our behavior must begin with avoiding self-disparagement.

## RATE ONLY BEHAVIOR

Self-disparagement begins with telling ourselves that, because we behaved badly, *we* are bad. Thus, if we wish to succeed at *teshuvah,* we must stop evaluating ourselves poorly because of our poor conduct.

We assess ourselves out of a need to prove our worth, both to ourselves and to others. We strive mightily to avoid making any errors, to maintain a good rating. If we manage our children well, we rate ourselves highly. When we cope poorly, however, we give ourselves a low rating. Our children's misconduct will also trigger negative evaluation. We reason, "If I did everything right, my children would always behave perfectly." Therefore we judge ourselves as bad parents whenever our children misbehave.

Such striving for perfection to prove our worth is wasteful and uncalled for. Perfection is not a requirement. While we might well prefer to be perfect, it is simply impossible. As Torah observes, no one can be perfectly righteous.

Above all, judgment is God's domain and not our business. It is best to give up global evaluation of ourselves, and concentrate instead on particular traits and behavior. "I acted badly," not "I'm a bad mother"; "I have a bad habit of getting angry," not "I am bad because I get angry." Again, we must separate the deed from the doer. When we have learned to stop thinking of ourselves as bad people because of our faulty behavior, we will no longer feel destructively guilty.

Changing those inner messages is a major factor in eliminating harmful self-disparagement. Reproaches such as "I was such a stupid idiot when I . . ." or "No one else would have been so selfish as to . . ." are intolerant and negative self-evaluations. A negative view of ourselves leads us to believe that we will always fail in this manner, and reinforces the very behavior we are trying so hard to change. By substituting more objective and less accusatory language, such as "It was improper to . . ." or "It would have been better to . . ." or "I haven't been very . . ." we are less likely to judge ourselves. Our emphasis should be on self-acceptance, along with an acknowledgment that we could do better. Instead of "How terrible of me to get so angry!" tell yourself, "It wasn't proper to get angry; I'll try to control myself better next time." Rather than "I should be more patient!" think, "I haven't been very patient, but I'll try to improve."

Once we have taken this step, we should focus on any irrationality in our statements. For example, "I should be more patient!" often implies an exaggerated expectation. We would

21

have to be angels to be perfectly patient all the time.

We might also question the validity of our descriptions. "Why am I *always* yelling at my children?" is an obvious exaggeration; it is unlikely that any parent yells at his children *all* the time.

Often, however, we criticize ourselves when in truth we have done nothing wrong at all. For instance, we call ourselves "mean" when, in fact, we acted in our child's best interest. Some of us manage to find fault with ourselves all the time. Nothing we do seems to be right or enough. If we were strict, we think we should have been more lenient. If we have been lenient, we tell ourselves we should have been stricter. If you have this habit, ask yourself, the next time you feel guilty: Did I really do anything wrong? If you did, do *teshuvah* for it. But if you didn't, why in the world are you feeling guilty?

Another insidious source of guilt and self-denigration is comparison. Many mothers constantly compare their performance with that of other mothers to see how they measure up. When they see a neighbor succeed better in some area, they conclude, "She is a better mother than I am."

Comparison of ourselves to others in terms of worth is harmful. It is, of course, possible to learn from others' exemplary behavior. If I notice that my neighbor is especially patient with her children, I can learn skills from observing her. Such modeling is only effective, though, after first eliminating all comparison.

Rating ourselves highly implies the possibility of rating ourselves poorly as well. While our self-esteem may get a boost from a high rating for good actions, it inevitably takes a beating when our rating falls because of poor performance. The only permanent solution to the problem of our low self-esteem is to stop rating ourselves altogether.

As for our actual worth, this should not be our concern. No one is capable of determining his own, or anyone else's true worth; this must be left to God. It is sufficient for us to know that every individual possesses great potential worth, by virtue of his having been created in God's image.[28] Indeed, our sages teach that a person should always tell himself: "The world was created for my sake."[29]

## IMPLEMENTING *TESHUVAH*

Once we have given up non-constructive self-criticism and self-denigration, we can begin the difficult task of correcting our bad habits. Remember, when we do *teshuvah* for bad habits, regret should *follow* correction. First, we must concentrate on concrete efforts to change.

The first step is to recognize that most bad habits stem from lack of self-control. The essential root of this problem is our demand to have everything our way. Whenever we display some destructive trait, it can be traced to this demand. For example, when we get angry at a child for disobedience, underlying the anger is our demand, "My children *must* obey me! (and I can't stand it when they don't!)." When we make selfish choices, we act from the belief that we *must* have comfort and convenience (and cannot bear it when we don't!). Therefore, we elevate our needs over those of others. Once we realize this, we can gradually give up such demands. The key word is "gradual." We are dealing here with fundamental personality change, and that takes time.

Only after we have measurably diminished our faulty traits should we begin to regret our past. Regret at this point, writes Rabbi Schlessinger, will not depress us. On the contrary, it develops and elevates the soul by cleansing it of the harmful after-effects of our transgression. The extent of regret that this requires is a matter of individual judgment. In any event, after spending Yom Kippur in sincere regret, we may be confident that our transgressions will be forgiven.[30] Indeed, if we confess and repent a transgression on Yom Kippur and then continue to worry about it, this implies a lack of faith in God's promise to grant us atonement.[31] Moreover, such

23

continued preoccupation with our guilt may interfere with our functioning.[32]

Reminding ourselves of our earlier transgressions and reexperiencing the pain of regret over them can reinforce our resolve not to repeat them. This is therefore recommended for subsequent Days of Atonement. However, it is inadvisable to let this interfere with the joy and optimism of our daily life.[33]

## APOLOGIZING TO CHILDREN

Parents often wonder whether it is wise or proper to apologize to their own child when they have hurt him unnecessarily. Part of the *teshuvah* process, after all, is to ask for forgiveness from those we have wronged.[34]

Rabbi Wasserman says that parents definitely should apologize to their child in such situations, and that it will improve their relationship with him. However, one must know how to apologize. It should not be done guiltily; it is best to say something like, "I shouldn't have screamed at (hit) you before. I'm sorry about it." The child must know that anger is wrong. If our inappropriate anger toward him is overlooked, we are in effect teaching him that it is all right for him to get angry too.

When we apologize to our children, we are also modeling *modeh al haemeth* (admitting wrongdoing). This is a most effective method of teaching our children how to recognize their own mistakes and apologize. It sets an example for them to remember and follow.

## INTERACTIONS OF GUILT AND ANGER

While guilt is often a reaction to anger, it can also trigger it. For example, when we see perpetual disorder in our children's room, we may jump to the conclusion that we are failures for not getting them to be neat. We then turn on the children in anger — blaming them for making us into failures.

We have to recognize that the source of such anger is our

guilt feelings. What sets the anger off is thinking, "They make me feel like such a failure! (I am a failure)." The only way to eliminate this kind of anger is to stop blaming ourselves for our poor parenting skills. Instead, we should do what we can to improve, and in the meantime be patient with both ourselves and our children.

Some parents find themselves in a vicious cycle of anger and guilt. When they feel guilty for getting angry at their child, they react by blaming the child for their anger *and* their guilt — and become even angrier at the child. "It's all his fault!" they tell themselves. "If *he* hadn't behaved so badly, *I* wouldn't have had to get angry, and wouldn't be suffering these terrible guilt feelings now!" What fuels the anger in this situation is an inability to tolerate guilt feelings and the demand that they go away. It is another example of low frustration tolerance. In this cycle, anger triggers guilt, which triggers further anger. After several repetitions, the cycle can raise our anger to a veritable crescendo. To stop the process, we must learn to tolerate the pain of our guilt feelings, as long as they still plague us.

## GUILT OVER GUILT

There are parents who are fully aware of their useless habit of constantly telling themselves off, and realize that they cause themselves senseless misery this way. However, they then proceed to berate themselves even more mercilessly for behaving so stupidly, making themselves yet more miserable. "Why do I torture myself with this constant self-criticism? Why don't I stop it, and change my behavior instead!" Such secondary guilt feelings are even more pernicious and difficult to uproot than the original guilt.

These parents should keep in mind that, like any other bad habit, this habit, too, is difficult to change. If they want to succeed at behavior change, they first must learn to stop telling themselves off for substituting guilt for self-improvement.

## GUILT ABOUT NOT GIVING ENOUGH ATTENTION

Because so much has been written about giving children sufficient attention, many parents have become anxious about it. Mothers in particular tend to suffer from guilt on this score.

While severe neglect is of course harmful, children do not require nearly as much attention as some professionals would have us believe. In fact, giving a child constant, excessive attention can lead to a demanding child. If told quietly and with a smile "I'm busy now — in a few minutes I'll have time for you," children can learn to wait until the parent is free to tend to their needs. A child who keeps calling from another room "Mommy, Mommy!" can be answered with "I can't come right now — I'm busy with . . ." Thus the child learns to accept with equanimity that he cannot always have your attention.

Mothers are sometimes told that they must give each child some "special" time when he has his mother's undivided attention. A mother who makes her child feel that he is accepted and loved, and who, when she listens to him, does so exclusively, need not go out of her way to give him such special time.

## GUILT OF THE WORKING MOTHER

A mother who works outside the home may worry that she harms her children by being away from them for substantial parts of the day. She might even judge herself a bad mother and feel guilty.

The mother's plight is real. She would like to spend more time with her children, but she cannot. However, her guilt is out of place. Judging ourselves, whether for real or imagined harm we cause our children, is always destructive.

If the mother must work, the best thing she can do for herself and her children is to make peace with her decision.

## LEARNING TO ACCEPT OURSELVES

Parents who have read about the harmful effects of parental mismanagement may exaggerate the "awfulness" of it. They may believe that whenever they lose control, they inflict irreparable damage on the child. After a display of anger, they are likely to think in horror, "How awful! Look what I'm doing to my children!" Parents who suffered as children from *their* parents' anger, and who resolved never to cause their own children similar suffering, tend to feel particularly guilty about their anger. They tell themselves, "I said I would never do this to *my* children, yet here I am doing it anyway!"

There is, of course, no denying the possibility of harmful consequences to the child when parents are in poor control. However, "awfulizing" and feeling guilty about this is destructive and does nothing to improve the situation. A noted psychologist comments:

> We have been subjected to abuses by parents throughout the ages and if human nature were not so strong as it is, what would have become of all of us? It is true that we could have been better and that we should try to help our children to become better and happier human beings. But one factor in helping them is to recognize their ability to withstand so many of the bad influences which we exert on them, unwillingly and unconsciously.[35]

It may help us to better accept ourselves if we downgrade the "awfulness" of what we ourselves suffered from our parents' anger. Our pain did not stem from their anger, but from our evaluation of it. As young children, we did not know how to protect ourselves from our parents' anger. When they became angry at us, we jumped to the conclusion that we were bad. We failed to make the necessary distinction between our basic nature and our behavior. So we concluded that we were bad and unworthy of being loved. This was the true source of our suffering at that time.

It is, of course, very discouraging to repeat the same mistakes our parents made. It is normal, though, during a stressful situation, to automatically revert to the patterns we saw acted out when we were children. It is no easy matter to change these automatic reactions.

For some of us, change may be so exceptionally difficult that we become convinced we are truly incapable of it. This is *never* true. People can and do learn new ways of reacting. But we will continue to feel sure we cannot change as long as we keep telling ourselves so. The message repeats itself in our head like a tape being played over and over: "I *can't* change; it's *too* hard; it's *too* much work; I *won't* be able to do it; I give up." We must change this recording for a new one; one that is more encouraging in its message. "I *can* change. It's difficult, but I'll keep trying and I *won't* give up. It may be hard work, but I'm prepared for it."

Thus, in order to change, we must believe in our ability to do it. We must also be sufficiently motivated to undertake the hard work necessary to succeed. We can draw strength from our belief in the God-given capacity for change, and from our faith that He who endowed us with this divine attribute will grant us the wisdom and strength to exercise it as well.[36]

In the meantime, remember that the minute we become aware of our larger mistakes, they are no longer failures in parenting. They become the steps of the process of becoming better parents. *Good judgment comes from experience, and experience comes from poor judgment.* So we can profit from our mistakes, rather than criticize ourselves for them.

## A WORD OF CAUTION

Reading this book, or any other guide, is only a beginning. Understanding parenting principles is relatively easy. Changing our behavior is slow and difficult. Don't feel guilty when, despite all your new knowledge, you continue to get upset. Don't tell yourself, "I'm not supposed to let anything upset me anymore; I should be able to keep myself calm by controlling my thinking!" While you may have a good understanding of cognitive principles, it does not mean that you will always make use of them. It is unreasonable to demand that because you have learned these concepts, you will be able to apply them at all times. Emotional habits such as anger and guilt are difficult to eliminate, even when we possess effective techniques for doing so. While we may go far in freeing ourselves of them, it is unlikely that we will ever succeed in eradicating them completely.

# The Mitzvoth of Honor and Reverence for Parents

## a. Nature of the Mitzvah

The obligation to honor and revere father and mother is fundamental to Judaism. It is included among the first five commandments, which deal with man's relationship to God, rather than among the last five which have to do with man's relationship to his fellow man. From this we learn, say our sages, that honoring one's parents is comparable to honoring God Himself.[1]

Honor of parents is linked to honor of God in another way. Torah views both the parents and God as partners in the child's creation. Honor of parents is thus equated with honor of God. "There are three partners to [the creation of] a man: God, his father, and mother. When a man honors his father and his mother, God says, 'It is as if I dwelled among them and they honored Me.'"[2]

The child's debt to his parents is not merely physical, but spiritual as well. It is the parents who transmit the Torah heritage to their child. Thus they become the child's link to the divine source of revelation.

In short, a child's parents are roots of both his physical existence and his spiritual existence. That is why the child is commanded to honor and revere them.

## Gratitude

At the heart of the commandment to honor and revere parents is gratitude. For the child, this involves a sense of appreciation for his parents' share in bringing him into the world, and for the love, concern, and sacrifice they extend in caring for him. In other words, the child must learn to recognize the good he receives from his parents in order to properly revere and honor them.

As time goes on, this capacity for gratitude will extend to God himself.

> It is only proper that he render them all the honor and do them all the service he can. For they brought him into the world and they labored greatly on his behalf during his childhood. Once a man has acquired this trait, he will ascend from it to be grateful for the good done him by God, who is the cause of his being and the cause of the existence of all his forefathers, reaching back to Adam.[3]

Thus, teaching a child to show gratitude to his parents becomes the foundation not only of honor and reverence, but also of the love of God which is central to religious life. This explains why a sense of gratitude is so strongly emphasized in Jewish ethical writings. It lends additional weight to the parents' obligation to initiate their children into the mitzvoth of honor and reverence.

## The Difficulties

This does not mean that teaching gratitude is easy. Young children are naturally self-centered, and it is difficult to instill in them any awareness of their parents' efforts. From their earliest years children are accustomed to enjoying their parents' favors and devotion, and they take this care for granted. They will often fail to appreciate to what extent their parents take pains for them. Consequently children usually lack that gratefulness which would motivate them to honor their parents.

Even if children are aware of all the things their mothers and fathers do for them, they may attribute such behavior to paternal and maternal instincts and thereby deny that there is any real dedication and sacrifice to be thankful for.

In addition, every child has a developing desire for independence. Hence children may perceive their parents' educational efforts as an attempt at domination. They may resent parental authority and even resist it. It is often hard for them to accept the restrictions and requirements which parents must impose.

Because of the difficulties in teaching honor and reverence, it is especially important to emphasize that we require the child to honor and revere us *for his own benefit*. This means we must try to avoid reacting with anger or hurt feelings when our children do not show proper respect or fail to obey us. We want the welfare of the child to be the focus of attention, not our own feelings.

Thus, when they speak to their child about disrespectful conduct, parents should be careful that he does not get the impression they are merely promoting their personal honor. One way of avoiding this impression is for one parent to speak to the child about any improper behavior toward the other parent.[4] Requests for apologies can also be handled in this way. For example, the father might gently urge the child, "Go tell your mother you're sorry and ask her to forgive you."

It is also important to keep in mind that revering and honoring one's parents is a two-way responsibility. That is, while children have an obligation to revere and honor their parents, it is up to the parents to create an atmosphere where reverence and honor come easily. It is forbidden for parents to overburden their child, as this could cause him to falter in revering and honoring them. Instead, parents should be forgiving and, occasionally, even look away. As the Shulchan 'Arukh states:

The father is forbidden to impose too heavy a yoke on his children, to be too exacting with them in matters pertaining to his honor, lest he cause them to stumble. Rather he should forgive them and shut his eyes; for a father has a right to forego the honor due him.[5]

Rabbi Aryeh Leib, eldest son of the famed Chafetz Chaim, writes of his father's educational approach to his children, "We were cautioned little pertaining to honor due our parents ... he related to us as to a friend and brother."[6] Parents who neglect to give proper respect to their child create a great obstacle to the child's respect for them. Conversely, parents who show sufficient respect and honor to their children are paving the path for their children to observe the mitzvoth of honoring and respecting parents. The atmosphere in the home is deeply influential. Modeling the way to act will always be the most powerful form of education.

Naturally, the way parents behave toward each other also serves as a model. Husbands and wives must talk to each other respectfully. This is, of course, a mitzvah in itself. But it also sets the standard for interaction in the family. Snide remarks, criticism, yelling, joking at each other's expense, interrupting each other, and other forms of disrespect between the parents usually reappear in the behavior of their children. Children are very observant and learn by imitation; so it is best to give them something worth imitating.

While occasional disagreement on childrearing issues is normal, it is not for the children's consumption. In particular, one parent should never criticize the other's handling of some discipline problem (nor, for that matter, anything else) in the children's presence; all differences should be worked out in private.

In general, the husband and wife are partners in the childrearing endeavor and should cooperate at all times, giving each other support and advice.

## Defining the Mitzvah

The mitzvoth of honor and reverence for parents are based on two biblical verses:

> 1. Honor your father and mother. . . .[7]
> 2. Every man his mother and father shall he revere. . . .[8]

The Gemarah defines honor and reverence as follows:

> Our Rabbis taught: What is reverence and what is honor? Reverence means that [the son] must neither stand nor sit in his [father's] place nor contradict his words, nor evaluate his opinions.
>
> Honor means that he must give him food and drink, clothe and cover him, and accompany him when he enters and leaves.[9]*

These descriptions should be taken as illustrations rather than comprehensive definitions. Honor and reverence are attitudes and the above merely manifestations of these attitudes. They are reflections of an inner feeling. The specific examples given in the Talmud are certainly meaningful, but a proper fulfillment of these mitzvoth consists of far more. The actual obligations are "too numerous to list and discussions of them would be overly long."[13] Indeed, our sages view honor and reverence for parents as knowing no limits.[14]

We will limit ourselves here to those aspects of the mitzvah with which parents must be familiar in order to teach it to the child.

---

* No significance should be attached to the fact that the masculine singular is used in this as well as other passages. The obligations of reverence and honor apply to daughters as well as to sons,[10] and mothers are to be accorded the same honor and reverence due to fathers.[11] The Mishnah deduces this from the above quoted verses.[12]

## What is Reverence?

Reverence basically means that the child is conscious of his parents' elevated status and dignity, and careful never to dishonor them in any way.[15] The mitzvah of reverence requires the child to see his parents as a "king and queen" whom he must be very careful not to offend.[16]

The halakhic authorities stress several formal expressions of reverence.

1. *Occupying the parents' place.* The child should not stand or sit in the place habitually occupied by his parents, either in the home or outside of it, such as in the synagogue.[17]

2. *Contradicting the parents' words.* The child may not contradict his parents, either in discussions on Torah or in general conversation. This applies only to explicitly contradictory statements; it is permissible for children to engage in debates with their parents on general topics, as well as Torah law. Children are allowed to present arguments which contest a parent's position as long as this is done respectfully.[18] Thus, for example, if the father says that it is permissible to read a newspaper on Shabbath, the son may not say that it is forbidden. He may, however, cite opinions which disallow it.

Even in a case where the child has been rebuked by mistake, he may not contradict the parent by saying "That's not true." Rather, he should try to set things straight by expressing himself in a non-contradictory way such as, "I can explain myself."[19]

3. *Evaluating the parents' opinions.* If a parent has a disagreement with someone else, the child may not decide in favor of either side. He may not even express endorsement for his parent's point of view by saying, for example, "My father is right."[20] It is arrogant for a child to set himself up as a judge of his parents' opinions.

4. *Calling parents by their name.* A child must not call his parent by name.[21] However, if someone asks him, "Whose son are you?" he is permitted to state his parent's name.[22] It is

also permissible for a child to write his parent's name.[23]

5. *Waking the parents.* A child is generally forbidden to wake his parents. If, however, the child knows that the father would want to be woken, as, for example, to prevent a financial loss, then he fulfills a mitzvah by waking him. Likewise, the child should wake his parents when it is necessary for the performance of a mitzvah, such as synagogue worship.[24]

The Bible pronounces a curse on anyone who treats his parents lightly or shows them contempt in any way.[25] In the words of Rambam:

> For anyone who treats his father or mother with contempt, even if by mere word or gesture, is cursed out of the mouth of God.[26]

Included in this category is one who causes his parents distress.[27]

## What is Honor?

The essence of honor is that the child hold his parents in high esteem and regard them as persons of great worth and importance. Honor expresses itself in thought, word, and action.[28] Primarily, it obligates the child to render his parents personal service, as befits persons of great worth and importance. He should tend to their needs and serve them in all the ways a servant serves his master.[29]

The obligation to provide for the parents' basic needs applies even when they do not make an explicit request. For example, if a child knows that his mother is thirsty he must bring her a drink. However, if it is not a basic need, the child must provide it only if the parent has actually asked for it.[30]

From the Talmud's definition of honor quoted earlier, we see that it includes both the satisfaction of physical needs, such as food, drink, and clothing, and symbolic gestures of attentiveness, such as accompanying the parents when they come and leave.

We also find a revealing reference in the Talmud to the manner of service:

> Rabbi Shimeon ben Gamliel said, "I served my father all my life, but I did not extend to him even one-hundredth of the honor given Isaac by Esau. For I would serve my father dressed in dirty clothes, and when I would go to my affairs would change into clean clothes, but Esau always dressed as royalty to serve his father."[31]

Clearly, true honor goes beyond physical acts of personal service. It also involves the manner of performing the service: the positive and caring attitude and the extra thoughtfulness.

## Obedience

Even though there is no general statement making obedience part of the mitzvoth of honor and reverence, it is largely implied in these mitzvoth. A disobedient child who acts contrary to his parents' expressed wish, or fails to do as he is asked, is being disrespectful and thus transgresses the mitzvah of reverence: "If the son does not obey his father, it is the same as if he contradicted him."[32] Others see the fear of transgressing the parents' requests as part of reverence.[33]

On the other hand, many of the things which parents ask of a child, such as helping with housework or going on an errand, are acts of service from which the parent derives benefit. Such acts of obedience are thus a form of honor. Indeed, Rabbi Akiva Eger points out that even when the request does not relate to personal service, granting a parent the satisfaction of having his wish done is a fulfillment of the mitzvah of honor.[34]

# b. Teaching the Mitzvah

If children are to properly extend honor and reverence to their parents, they must be taught the various laws pertaining to these mitzvoth. Ideally, the child should learn these at school. No matter how much the parents emphasize their concern for their child, and no matter how careful they are to be objective, the child may still think they are asking for respect and honor out of their own self-interest. It will always be somewhat awkward for a parent to say, "This is how you have to treat me." It is simply easier for outsiders to teach these attitudes.

This does not mean, however, that parents should in any way hesitate to explain aspects of the mitzvah when they feel it is necessary.

## Teaching Reverence

Parents should make sure that even their very young children show respect toward them. This is important not only for the parent-child relationship but also for the child's developing attitude toward others. It is in his dealings with his own mother and father that the child learns how to behave toward people in general. Moreover, if parents permit a child to acquire habits of disrespect toward them while he is still young, they may find it extremely difficult to change this behavior pattern as the child grows older.

No matter how careful we ourselves may be in modeling respectful behavior for our children, they will still at times show disrespect toward us. Sadly, the environment provides them with plenty of models of disrespectful behavior. Moreover, every child is bound to be displeased with his parents on occasion; perhaps they have imposed some restriction or required him to do something he does not like. At these times he is likely to behave disrespectfully.

If we want to deal effectively with such behavior, we must

try to view the situation objectively. This means avoiding reacting with anger ("How dare he talk to me this way!"), personal hurt ("How awful that *my own child* talks to me like this!"), or guilt ("Where have I failed that my child speaks to me with such disrespect!"). Our reaction should be, instead, one of concern: "The child's behavior is bad for him. Let me see how I can best handle the problem." However, parents do not have to keep their feelings completely neutral. Sometimes a show of mild hurt can move the child toward regret. It may be enough merely to say the child's name softly, with a slightly disappointed look on your face. Also, quietly telling him (but not often) that we feel bad because of the way he spoke to us can have a good effect on him.

For the very young child, a mild reprimand, delivered quietly and lovingly, is usually sufficient. Taking the child's hand in his, the parent might say, "You're not allowed to talk to Daddy (Mommy) this way."

Young children will sometimes hit or bite their mother. Usually the child is merely playing, or testing to see his mother's reaction; sometimes he may be expressing anger. Whatever the reason for the child's behavior, the mother should not permit it. She should not hit or bite back (even if only to show what it feels like) but should quietly tell the child "No," holding up a finger for emphasis. If he keeps on doing it, it may be necessary to react more firmly. Hold the child's hand or take hold of his mouth as you tell him with great seriousness, "You are *not* allowed to hit your mother" ("You are *not* allowed to bite"). Children generally do not keep up such behavior for long.

With an older child who acts disrespectfully, it can be effective if, in our initial reaction, we ignore him. Suppose, for example, the child comes and says demandingly, "How come I don't have any clean socks?" We give no answer, but turn away to occupy ourselves in some way. When the child continues to ask about his socks, we can ask, quietly, "Do you know why I'm not answering you? Maybe you don't realize it but the way you spoke to me was disrespectful. You're not allowed to complain to your parents that way. Now, if you need clean socks and there aren't any in the drawer, how could you come and tell me about this in a pleasant way?" (If you have overlooked such disrespect in the past, you might say, "I know I haven't corrected you on this before but from now on I will point it out to you.")

Similarly, a child who screams at his parents should be ignored for the moment. When he has calmed down somewhat the parent might say, making sure to keep his voice low, "I know you were upset before, but you know, you're not allowed to scream at me. You can tell me you're upset and that something is bothering you, but you must tell it to me quietly."

Be especially careful not to defend yourself or offer explanations when the child complains to you disrespectfully. Parents frequently forget themselves in such situations and proceed to argue with the child. They don't realize that by overlooking his disrespect in this way, they are in effect sanctioning it. To act as effective educators, we must set aside for the moment the issue raised by the child, and first deal with his disrespect. For example, a child may complain at mealtime, "You're always giving him first!" Here we might answer, "I can see you're unhappy, but that's no way to tell it to me. What could you say instead?" (pause) "Mommy, could you give me first sometimes too?" A youngster may grumble, "How come (so and so's) parents let him buy himself something when he goes to the grocer for them and you don't!" The parents' first response should not be a defensive explanation such as, "This is the way things are done in our house." Instead, they should quietly point out to the child that he is not permitted to complain about his parents' decisions in this way. The issues of fairness and comparison should only be dealt with after the issue of speaking respectfully. It is acceptable for children to ask for something, but not if they imply that their parents are not doing things properly.

Be careful also not to overlook any showing of annoyance

toward us by the child, such as, "Okay, okay, I heard you."

One mother describes the effect on her eleven-year-old daughter's disrespectful habits, after she developed a clear but loving way of correcting her.

> Esther was getting more and more "chutzpadik." She was really talking to me like I was a child or worse, like I just didn't count. I found myself getting angrier and angrier. She complained about my cooking, about my asking her to help with chores, about having to keep her room in order — everything. Once I really hit her hard across the face, after which I felt just awful. It was so unpleasant to be around her. At our weekly group meeting it was suggested that I hold her hand and say things like, "You know, you have a very bad habit of talking to your father and me in an unkind and disrespectful manner. I know you can control yourself. I'm sure you don't like being like this." It really worked — the hand holding especially. Esther was very much affected by that. She would become very contrite and apologize. She told me that she knew that what she was doing was wrong, but that "I just couldn't control myself." I assured her that though it might be difficult, she could learn to control herself. It was just a matter of changing a bad habit. Esther was really sorry. Before this, when I yelled, she would just yell back and act even worse.

Once children learn about respect, they may frequently feel unhappy and regretful after having shown disrespect. In such a case reprimands are unnecessary. It is enough to tell the child, "I know you're sorry about the way you talked to me before." Children are likely to tell us they are sorry on their own more and more often, as they become more aware of their disrespectful behavior.

Parents often unwittingly contribute to the problem of

disrespect by arguing back when their child contradicts them. Remember, a child is not allowed to directly contradict his parents. They should be very careful not to push him further into transgression. For example, if the child responds to something the parent says with "That's not true," the parent should not argue back, allowing the disagreement to grow into a debate where parent and child take turns defending their position. For the moment, refraining from answering at all is often the best way to handle the situation. Correcting the child on the spot by telling him "You're contradicting me" will most likely only result in sullen resentment.

Sometime later, when defensiveness is at a minimum, the parents can correct the child for disagreeing with them. They should try to do so lovingly and without any hint of criticism or reproach. This is the opportunity to model appropriate ways for a child to express dissent. A father might explain: "Here is how you can tell me if I said something which appears to you to be incorrect — 'Daddy, you said Aunt Rivkah is coming to visit on Monday. I thought I heard her say that she would come on Tuesday.'"

Remember, in correcting a child for disrespect, it is essential that we keep our voice low. This way we convey our love and concern, our most powerful tools for changing behavior.

If a child's disrespectful behavior becomes more serious or persistent, it may be necessary to resort to punishment (see Chapter 5, "Punishment for Disrespect").

## Teaching Honor

Parents should provide opportunities and encourage their child to do things for them. They should not hesitate, for example, to ask him to bring them a glass of water, or to send him on some errand. It is a nice practice for the father to ask the child to do things for the mother, and vice versa. Thus the mother might say to the child, "Please bring Daddy this cup of tea I prepared for him."

A natural opportunity to train children in the observance of their mitzvah presents itself regularly at mealtimes. The leisurely Shabbath meals are especially suited for this training. Recently we were guests at a home where we had the pleasure to watch two small children, a boy of four and a girl of six, serve nearly the entire Shabbath noon meal with obvious pride and pleasure, virtually unaided by the mother. Most impressive of all, the children did what was necessary without being told, which included clearing the table after each course. Obviously, some perseverance is needed to bring children to such a level. In the long run, however, the results make it worth our while.

## Teaching Obedience

As mentioned earlier, obedience is an aspect of the mitzvoth to honor and revere parents. It is also the tool that enables parents to train the child, helping him acquire the self-control which he needs in order to develop all other positive character traits. Finally, obedience to parents prepares the child to obey God, which is the foundation of Jewish life.

Important as it is, obedience cannot be forced on children. Parents who simply keep insisting "You *have* to do it" are bound, sooner or later, to encounter resistance. Though obedience to parents is required by Torah law, parents who demand it of the child as their right — reminding him frequently of his duty — are likely to only arouse resentment. Similarly, while punishment can be used to force a child to obey, continual use of this method is also sure to backfire.

How, then, do we make the child obey? Rabbi Simcha Wasserman points out, "We cannot make people do what we want them to do, but we can make people *want* to do what we want."[35] Here is the answer. We must concentrate our efforts on instilling in the child the *desire* to obey us. This willing cooperation can only evolve if the parents' demands are based on loving concern, sincere respect, patience, and moderation.

## LOVING CONCERN

A child is quick to sense it if his parents are demanding obedience for their personal convenience. He will learn from their example to place his interests first, too. If they are to succeed in their training, the parents' primary motivation must be genuine concern for the child's welfare. When the child senses such loving concern, it will encourage him to obey us, simply because he knows that to do so is for his good. He will have confidence that caring and consideration for him underlies any demands we make.

## SINCERE RESPECT

Parents must treat their child with the same respect they would want for themselves. The Sages teach, "Let the honor of your pupil be as dear to you as your own."[36] Rabbi Samson Raphael Hirsch comments on this that parents who demand honor and obedience but do not grant the child respect and dignity are bound to fail.[37]

## PATIENCE

At times, a child's balkiness stems from his resentment over the annoyance we show when he does not comply with our wishes. Learning to keep our negative reactions under control is an important part of teaching children obedience.

In particular, nothing gains a child's cooperation as much as a soft and gentle voice. In the classic *Igereth HaRamban*, the Ramban wrote to his son, "Always speak to people in a low tone of voice," adding that this will stop us from growing angry. A quiet voice is soothing; it creates that relaxed atmosphere which is so reassuring to the child and makes him feel much more inclined to do as we ask. When we speak quietly, we also convey strength; it is obvious that we are in control of ourselves and the situation. Parents who have worked on reducing the volume of their voice report that it has a dramatic effect on their children's behavior. As one mother related:

> Now that I have been trying out and using my newly learned skills in talking to my three-year-old son, I feel so much more in control because I can get him to do (or not to do) just about anything I want. All I do is just softly repeat my request (a few times if necessary) and he eventually comes through.

## MODERATE DEMANDS

Children are unlikely to cooperate if parents are excessive in their demands. Impositions should be made thoughtfully and kept within reasonable limits. If they are arbitrary or unnecessarily severe, parents become dictators rather than educators. Rabbi Hirsch writes:

> Never ask a child to do something unnecessary and unimportant; similarly, don't refuse a harmless and trivial request. But if you give an instruction, you must insist on its fulfillment, and if you have refused a request, you must stand by your refusal, despite all pleading and pressure on the part of the child. . . . Be careful with the word "No!" Let your child do and have whatever you can permit him, on the condition that it won't endanger his physical and moral wellbeing. . . .
>
> The manner in which we prohibit or permit, and the joy in which we grant the child the freedom to do as he pleases, make it obvious to him that prohibiting and permitting are not the expression of an arbitrary mood, a desire to dominate, or simple stubbornness; but rather result from serious considerations.[38]

Children simply become balky and resistant when we place excessive restrictions and requirements upon them. Getting children to be more obedient often involves reducing our demands on them. This means learning to stay calm and not worrying about everything having to be a certain way. It means learning to think mainly of the child's welfare rather than of our own immediate needs. Once we develop more inner calm and expect less perfection, we can overlook many more things. It becomes less necessary to impose so many burdens on the children. Again, we can help ourselves stay calm by learning to speak in a quiet and gentle voice.

## FOLLOWING THROUGH

Still, as Rabbi Hirsch advises, whenever we do ask something of the child we must make sure that he does it, and whenever we do refuse him something we must not let him have it, no matter how hard he tries to make us change our mind. It may, at times, be tempting to overlook disobedience as a way of avoiding conflict. In the end, this undermines our authority. For example, if we tell the child "No standing on the bus seats" and then ignore him when he does it anyway, we teach him that he doesn't have to listen to what we say. If we want the child to take our words seriously, we must follow through at all times.

We minimize our demands not simply to be permissive, but to render the demands we do make more potent and meaningful.

Finally, to be able to effectively set limits, we must know what can be expected of our child in terms of his age and level of development. Parents who are unsure about this ought to discuss it with other, more experienced parents.

## BEGINNING WITH BABIES

A wise parent will "childproof" the house when a baby first begins to crawl, putting breakable and dangerous objects well out of the infant's reach. However, sooner or later we must teach him that there are some things he must let alone.

We can't stop the baby by merely saying "No," at least not at first. He must learn what the word means. It is best, as soon as he goes for some forbidden object, to go over and quickly whisk him to another part of the room. As you do this, say "No" in a serious but non-threatening voice. Give him something interesting to distract him. However, if he continues to try to get at the object, take him out of the room, while saying quietly, "Mommy (Daddy) said no." Don't threaten, scold, or hit the child. Quiet and firm action is all that is called for. The child should be confined to some other part of the house or the playpen for at least ten minutes, before you let him back. A children's gate installed at the door is good for keeping the child out, at the same time that it enables us to keep an eye on him. You may have to repeat this procedure several times, but if you can remain patient and calm during this training period, the child will eventually learn to obey your "No."

Parents often think their child disregards them deliberately. They notice his glances in their direction and conclude that he is fully aware what he is doing. It is far more likely that the child is simply testing his parents to see how they will react. Consistent handling is essential; then there will be no more reason for such testing.

Naturally, we have to expect some damage to our possessions while the child is young. Our reaction at such times is crucial. A serious and regretful expression makes the deepest impression on the child. We might say, rather sadly, for instance, "Daddy's book is torn — now he can't read it," or "The plate is broken — now we have to buy a new one."

When you have to take some forbidden object away from the child, try to find something else to offer him as an alternative. Tell him, "You can't play with that but you can have this instead."

Obviously, a much stricter standard is necessary when training children to avoid potentially dangerous situations; this requires immediate and decisive handling. A sharp word and even physical punishment, properly administered, may be appropriate. If, for example, a toddler has just run out into the street, the parent might shout "No!" and give him one sharp spank as he retrieves him. While parents may well feel anxiety in such situations, it is best not to show anger or hysteria but merely great concern for the child's safety. Back safely on the sidewalk, the parent can tell the child in a serious, very emphatic voice, "The street is dangerous. Cars can hurt you. Don't ever do that again."

It is relatively easy to teach a child to stay away from hot objects. The first time the child approaches anything hot, we take his hand and very quickly and lightly touch it to the hot object as we say emphatically, "Hot, hot, hot!" One or two such demonstrations are usually enough to result in a quick retreat when we only call out "Hot!"

Another problem in disciplining toddlers involves excursions and shopping errands. As long as the child is kept in his stroller, everything is fine. However, as soon as he is taken out, he begins to wander all over. Calling him often doesn't help. This situation calls for resolute handling.

The mother should take the child and firmly place her hand over his on the stroller bar. If he nevertheless breaks away, it is best to quietly strap him into the stroller for a while. He can be given another chance after ten minutes or so. His crying should be completely ignored, except perhaps for a brief "I'm sorry, but now you have to stay in the stroller for a while."

Similarly, there is no need for raised voices or arguments if the child does not want to leave the park when it is time to go home. To give the child time to get used to the idea, give a simple warning: "We will be going home in a couple of minutes." After the time has passed, tell the child in a friendly way, "We have to go home now." Pick him up and carry him away, or place him firmly in his stroller, and go off without further ado. While he may scream and thrash about in protest, don't let his carrying on shake your resolve.

## WHEN THE CHILD REFUSES TO OBEY

Parents should be careful not to overreact to their child's "No." Very young children sometimes use this word for the shock effect it has on the parent. It is best to avoid giving explanations or trying to reason with the child, and instead to completely ignore him and act as if he had never said it. For instance, if you tell the child "Come, it's time for your bath" and he says "No," just start undressing him and put him into the tub.

Parents can make things easier for the child by refraining from asking questions such as "Do you want to (have your supper) (get dressed)?", instead steering him through his routines in a matter-of-fact way. It also helps to be tactful. If your twenty month old is busy assembling a necklace of pop-it beads at lunchtime, you can let him carry some beads to the table and take them away as you hand him his spoon. As the child grows older and is less distractable, you can try to give a little friendly advance warning when possible, so that you don't have to suddenly pull him away from some exciting activity.

As parents develop confidence in their ability to handle their child, they will not panic at his "No." They will convey their authority while maintaining a calm manner. (For more on this subject, see Chapter 3.)

## ACCUSTOMING THE CHILD TO OBEDIENCE

Once children pass beyond the toddler stage, our expectations of them will become more complex. Our methods of enforcing those expectations will also become more subtle. A simple "No!" and bodily transfer of the child to another room is no longer appropriate. The task for the parent is to exercise full authority without subjugating the child.

To become accustomed to obedience, the child must be given a chance to practice it on his own. Forced obedience, induced by coercive methods, teaches the child very little and should be used only as a last resort. For example, if the child helps himself to cookies, candies, or other snack foods which he knows he is not allowed to take, it is better not to immediately put these out of his reach. A child can learn proper obedience only when he has a choice. Allow him to choose between sneaking the sweets or controlling himself. This choice should be taken away only after he has repeatedly disregarded our rules. Even then, he should be given fresh opportunities from time to time to behave appropriately. Thus we might say, "I'm putting the cookies back in the drawer. Let's see how well you are able to control yourself."

## WITHHOLDING PRIVILEGES

On the other hand, parents should not hesitate to withhold privileges if necessary. For instance, suppose a child who has neglected to do some chore comes to ask for a snack. He may be told, "You can have crackers as soon as you've (emptied the garbage)." Other privileges which can be withheld from the child might be that of listening to music or going to visit his friend. Some forcefulness and perseverance may be called for at times, but the results are well worth it. One mother, who had in the past resorted to either screaming or giving in to her child, told about her experiences when she began acting more firmly and consistently.

> We were just finishing lunch. Three-year-old Menachem was throwing the remains of his tunafish on the floor. The other children took oranges and went outside. As Menachem went to get his orange, I decided that this would be a good time to try the "new approach." "As soon as you pick up your tunafish from the floor, Menachem, you may have an orange," I said, closing the refrigerator. Menachem gave me one of his daring looks and walked over to the refrigerator,

opened it, and took out an orange. "As soon as you pick up the tunafish you may have an orange," I repeated, taking the orange from him. I was determined to keep my cool this time and not scream at him or pick up the tunafish myself, as I had been doing in the past. One more try from Menachem and one more repetition of my firm decision, and Menachem gave me the funniest look, picked up the tunafish and said, "Okay, now can I have an orange?" This was quite an encouraging beginning!

## GIVING DIRECTIONS

Many of the do's and don'ts which we issue during the course of the day can be avoided by giving the child information which allows him to figure out for himself what he should do. For example:

> "Muddy boots belong outside."
> "Clothes which are thrown on the chair get crumpled."
> "Your pants are down."

You can also point out what has to be done without placing yourself at the center of the request. For example, instead of "I want you to go to bed" — "Time for bed." Rather than "I want this room cleaned up" — "The room has to be cleaned up." Speak quietly but unhesitatingly, using a minimum of words. Let your manner of speaking convey to the child that you expect compliance.

When it is necessary to restrict children, there is no reason to warn or threaten them. State the limitation quietly but firmly; whenever possible, give a brief reason for it. Here are examples:

> "No jumping on the sofa — it ruins the material."
> "I can't let you run around here at the bus stop — it disturbs the other people."

"No sand throwing — it can get into someone's eyes."

If children don't listen, take action to restrain them. For example, the child running around at the bus stop must now sit down with you or hold your hand. The toddler throwing sand is whisked out of the sandbox and quietly told, "Come, you'd better sit down next to me on the bench for a while." If necessary, hold on to him to prevent him from going back.

## GETTING CHILDREN TO COME WHEN CALLED

Many parents have trouble getting their child to come when he is called. If he doesn't come by the third time they go after him scolding, "How many times do I have to call you before you come!" While this may get results, the child, unfortunately, will learn to ignore his parents until they yell.

To teach the child that he must come when called, we first have to learn to control our angry reaction. The way to do this is to identify and change the thoughts which produce our anger, namely, "I shouldn't have to call him so many times to come. He should come right away!" We must be tolerant of the child's behavior, while at the same time working to change it.

Make it a practice not to call a child more than once. If he does not come, do not continue to call but go to him and tell him quietly, "When I call you, you have to come right away" or "You know, I called you." A mild rebuke such as "It's not right for you to ignore me when I call" might sometimes be in order.

Naturally, we should give the child a minute or so, and not expect him to come the instant we call. We can explain to him that when it is difficult for him to come right away, he can call out, "Just a minute please." Even when the child is playing outside, we should not keep calling him. It may be inconvenient to have to leave the house, but we must be prepared to suffer some inconvenience in order to achieve our educational goals.

## GET THE CHILD'S ATTENTION

Parents should avoid shouting instructions from one end of the house to the other. Many children have developed the habit of tuning their parents' voices out. If we want to be sure the child is attentive, we have to take the time to talk to him face to face. This way we are less likely to have to repeat what we say.

When a child acts as if he hasn't heard us, it is not always necessary to repeat ourselves. Instead, we can find out whether he got our message. For example:

> Mother: Naomi, please take the laundry out of the washing machine and put it into the dryer.
> Naomi: (doesn't answer and continues reading)
> Mother: (quietly) Naomi, what did I just say?
> Naomi: (looking up) Oh, you asked me to put the laundry into the dryer.
> Mother: Right. So please do it now.

## REMINDERS

Another way to encourage obedience is by well-placed reminders. For instance, we might tell a daughter who habitually postpones doing what she was asked, "Rebecca, would you set the table, and please remember what I said about not putting off jobs that need to be done right away."

## CORRECTION AND PUNISHMENT

Proper and appropriate correction is a major factor in gaining obedience. For example, if a child frequently neglects to do what is required of him, we might discuss with him the importance of complying promptly, explaining that this is part of the mitzvah of honoring parents, and that he gives his parents pleasure by fulfilling their requests eagerly. When a child responds to a request to do something by saying "I don't want to," he can be told, very quietly, "You know, children have to do what their Mommy and Daddy ask."

To teach a child that he must obey us, we may also need to use punishment at times (for more on this, see Chapter 5).

## A FINAL WORD

*Keep in mind that it takes time and patience to teach a child obedience.* It is important that we have realistic expectations. Remember that our children are not angels. Even the best behaved youngster will at times neglect to obey his parents. Don't generate anger in yourself by thinking, "Why can't he listen!" On the other hand, don't focus on thoughts of personal failure either ("What's wrong with *me* that I can't get him to listen!"). We need to maintain emotional control in order to calmly decide how best to handle the situation.

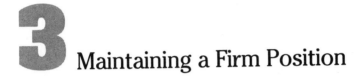

# Maintaining a Firm Position

To teach their children proper conduct and positive character traits, parents must be firm and consistent. But this is easier said than done. Parents may well understand the importance of being firm and consistent in handling their children, yet have great difficulty putting this theoretical knowledge into practice. They may know, for example, that it is not sensible to yield when a child cries over a refused request. Why, then, do they give in? Certain common fears and attitudes usually create the parents' difficulties. In this chapter we will try to understand these fears and attitudes, and the misconceptions on which they are based. By thinking more precisely about their way of handling their children, parents can begin to maintain a firmer and more consistent position.

## Concern About the Child's Happiness

Often, parents are not firm because they are afraid that the child will not be happy if he does not have things his way. This common fear stems from two false beliefs: 1) The goal of life is happiness, and it is the parents' job to make the child happy. This is expressed in the oft-heard, ". . . as long as he's happy." 2) The child must have what he wants in order to be happy.

## HAPPINESS

Of course we want our children to be happy. But it is a mistake to believe that it is our job to make them happy. The Torah requires the father to teach his son three things: Torah, a trade, and good character traits.[1] Nowhere does it say that he must make him happy. Why? Perhaps because by teaching him these things, he is giving the child all the tools he needs to be happy.*

Even if happiness were the most important thing in life, parents trying to make the child happy are bound to fail. Here is what the great nineteenth-century English philosopher, John Stuart Mill had to say on happiness:

> I have always felt that happiness is the touch-stone for all rules of behavior, and the purpose of life. But, I think now that the only way to be happy, is *not* to make of it the purpose of our activity. There is only one way to be happy; it consists of striving to any aim, but that of happiness itself. As to where pure pursuit of happiness, without moral moderation, leads the entire collective society — our generation has the unfortunate opportunity to witness it.

Modern educators emphasize the same basic idea:

> The goal of keeping a child happy will keep him from being a happy child. . . . So many mothers make the same mistake. They think the most important thing in raising children is to make them happy. It's

---

* Perhaps it is significant that there is no word for "happiness" in classical Hebrew. The term *osher*, translated as "happiness" in modern Hebrew, means "progress" in classical Hebrew. The closest term in classical Hebrew is *nachath ruach*, which literally means "rest of the spirit" and denotes peace of mind. Another term is *sameyach b'chelko*, "rejoicing in his lot." Both of these terms indicate a harmony between the individual's striving and reality. This, apparently, is how the Torah sees happiness.

not. If you raise your children to be dependable, industrious, honest and considerate of others, they will make themselves happy.[2]

## SATISFACTION OF DESIRES

Now to the second false belief — that in order to be happy, a child must have what he wants. Our sages were very astute observers, and found that "No one dies with half his wishes fulfilled. When he has one hundred, he wants to turn them into two hundred, and if he has two, he wants to make them into four hundred."[3] And the wisest of all men said, "One who loves money will never be satisfied with money."[4] A person can never have all he wants; and the child needs to learn this early in life.

Parents who satisfy their child's every wish to ensure his happiness might actually accomplish the very opposite. For the child who is used to getting what he wants may come to believe that it must always be this way. This need to have every wish fulfilled may lead to frequent unhappiness, since the parents are very likely to eventually become irritated over such demanding behavior. Moreover, later in life the child is likely to feel unhappy whenever he does not have what he wants. The happiness he experiences each time a desire is satisfied will be relatively short-lived, because it will not be long before the next as-yet-unfulfilled desire causes renewed and prolonged unhappiness. And there is still another reason not to overindulge the child.

> Although it sounds paradoxical, you actually cheat [the child] of pleasure when you give him too much. Pleasure occurs when an intense need is satisfied. If there is no need, there is no pleasure. . . . There are few conditions that inhibit a sense of appreciation more than for a child to feel he is entitled to whatever he wants, whenever he wants it.[5]

Remember that indulgence does not equal love. Modern psychology has gone to great lengths to stress the importance of parents showing love for their children, and has thereby done us real service. But when we equate love with granting of all wishes, we pervert this lesson. We show true love when we do what is good for the child. Restricting children when it is necessary is an important part of love, and it will not damage their affection for their parents if it is done in a caring and loving manner.

Moreover, when one of a child's wishes is denied by a loving parent and the child sees later that he is still happy, he learns a most fundamental lesson for life — that his happiness does not depend on getting what he wants. In the end, he will love and respect us for having taught him this wisdom.

To be sure, children may feel quite miserable when they are not permitted to have their way, especially if they have been indulged in the past. We can help them get over their unhappiness by conveying genuine empathy — a smiling face, gentle voice, and loving manner. The message to the child should be, "We limit you because we care about you. We are sorry if it causes you unhappiness."

## Avoidance of Conflict

Children frequently show their unhappiness over an unfavorable decision by complaining, crying, pouting, throwing accusing looks, and so on. Parents must be able to stand firm in the face of such resistance, no matter how unpleasant it may be. If they tell themselves that they "can't stand" the child's carrying on, they will find themselves, against their better judgment, giving in to him just to have their peace. Unfortunately, this only encourages the child to continue to resist the parents with unpleasant crying, nagging, and the like, since it gets him what he wants.

To avoid unpleasant fusses, parents will also say yes to the child when they really want to say no. Though they may succeed in avoiding immediate conflict, the child is likely to learn that his parents will let him have whatever he wants. In the long run the child becomes increasingly demanding, and the parents are forced to go to ridiculous lengths in order to avoid conflict.

Parents need to be aware of this problem so they can properly combat it. Rabbi Samson Raphael Hirsch advises:

> You must get used to suffering from a child's expressions of aggression, and not surrender in the face of screams. Don't give a child, because of self-love (so that he won't disturb your peace), what you wouldn't give him because of your love for him.[6]

Remember, too, that when we give in to our children, we deprive them of training in building up tolerance for the many frustrations they are bound to experience throughout life. It is worth learning to tolerate some unpleasantness now, because in the long run it will make things easier for everyone. When we stop giving in to children because of unpleasant carrying on, we may sometimes be quite surprised at the results. As this mother relates:

> Every evening I prepare the lunchboxes for my six children. Since by then I am usually very tired, I don't look forward to this job. In the past I'd asked my children to make the lunches, but they always argued and made such a fuss over the job that I would end up giving in.
>
> Armed with incentive from my workshop, I decided to try again. Each evening one of my four older children has the job to clear the supper table and tidy the kitchen. On Monday night at suppertime I made this announcement: "From now on, children, we're going to take turns making lunches. The one whose turn it is to clear the table and tidy up will also make lunches for everyone."

Immediately my ten year old Yossi, whose turn it was that evening to do the kitchen, began complaining in his usual manner. "Oh no, we can't do it — it takes too long — it's too hard! Especially not the night I clear, then I won't have time to play!"

"Yossi," I said, "tonight is your turn. I know it's not an easy job, but do it anyway." He continued to complain but I did not permit it to weaken my resolve. "Yossi, I know you don't like to. If it's too hard, I'll help. But please do it anyway."

Grumbling a little, he started the lunches. I pitched in, and sent everyone else out of the kitchen so only he and I could work together. He completed his job quite nicely.

The next night it was my daughter's turn. I didn't have to say a word. She began preparing lunches and needed almost no help.

The third night it was the turn of my eight-year-old son, who generally grumbles a lot. He had a class at yeshivah that evening which he was eager to attend. Right after supper he asked, "What should I make for sandwiches 'cause I have to leave soon."

I'd caused a minor miracle with only a small change in tactics!

## SHOPPING TRIPS

It is particularly difficult to remain firm and not give in when children ask us to buy them things on shopping trips. The child will say, "Buy me (candy, potato chips, a toy)" or "I want a..." Parents will typically answer, "No, you can't have any" or "No, I'm not buying you anything now." But the child continues to ask, often nagging relentlessly. Sometimes the parents manage to stand firm, but at other times they relent just to have their peace. Of course, this nicely reinforces the child's "buy me this" habit.

If they want to break this behavior pattern, parents must consistently refuse to give in, making absolutely no exceptions. It is best to tell the children, before going out with them, "Children, we are going to buy things we need for the house. Please don't ask me to buy you anything special." Then, if anyone forgets, remind him: "Remember what I said about not buying you things." Give no other answers or explanations. If the child pleads with you, simply ignore him. Naturally, this does not mean that the children will give up their habit right away. But if you stick to this approach, *never* responding at all to any requests except to say "Remember, we are buying things for the house now, and not special things for you," they will eventually stop. Then, when parents do want to give the child some small treat or toy, they can buy it when the child is not along and give it to him at home.

## TANTRUMS

If a child has learned to get what he wants by crying or screaming, it may be necessary to ignore his temper tantrums for some time, to teach him that this method will no longer work. A parent needs to have strong will power and considerable patience to resist a lengthy period of unpleasant noise and sometimes even kicking and thrashing about. Even a parent who is generally firm may be tempted to give in after the child persists in crying for a long time. Don't! Yielding after a while only teaches the child that if he keeps up his efforts long enough, he will get what he wants. The child will naturally reason, "They gave in before, maybe this time they'll give in again if I keep crying long enough." Therefore, the longer the crying has lasted, the more important it is not to give in to it.

However, we need not remain indifferent to the child's (albeit self-imposed) suffering. One can tell the child, "I'm very sorry, but I can't let you have what you want." In the case of a young child, a soothing hug given at the onset of a tantrum can often help him to get over it quickly.

## ABUSIVE BEHAVIOR

A child who is very angry and frustrated may, in order to get his way, scold and criticize his parents, throw objects or bang doors, curse and even become physically abusive. Such behavior can easily frighten the parents into submitting to all kinds of unreasonable demands. This, of course, only reinforces the child's low frustration tolerance and encourages further aggressiveness.

Again, though it may be difficult, parents must learn to stand firm and remain unaffected by the child's behavior. If he abuses his parents verbally, they should calmly explain that they will not listen to him if he speaks disrespectfully — and then ignore him until he calms down. If he damages objects, he should be quietly told to leave the room, or even the house if necessary, until he can control himself.

Physical attacks on parents are another matter. Since they are a serious transgression, the parents must stop the child by restraining him physically, with the help of other adults if necessary. This must be done without hostility; it should be clear that the parents act out of concern for the child's welfare. If parents focus on what needs to be done rather than on their feelings of hurt or anger, they will be able to maintain the calm but firm manner required.

Remember, the child is undoubtedly frightened by his own physical violence. It is also quite likely that he fears parental rejection because of his behavior. It is very important, therefore, that the parents demonstrate that they still care for him. While his behavior cannot be tolerated, they do not reject him because of it.

## What Will People Think?

When the child carries on in the presence of guests or in a public place, the parent sometimes worries, "What will these people think of me?" or "I can't let him bother all these people." The first of these worries stems from an exaggerated concern over the opinion of others. The other worry places concern for other people's inconvenience above the very fundamental educational needs of the child. In either case, the parent gives in to the child's demands, which temporarily stops the fussing and crying. The child, however, quickly learns that fussing in public gets him what he wants. He will make more and more demands, knowing that the parent fears the public disturbances he makes when his demands are not met.

Parents who are concerned about "what others will think" may find themselves overlooking all sorts of inappropriate behavior in order to prevent a temper tantrum. When we depend on the approval of others, we only undermine ourselves; there will always be someone who disapproves or disagrees with what we are doing. At one point or another, parents must turn a deaf ear to what anyone else is saying and hold on to their own priorities.

A child who throws a tantrum in public challenges the parent to exercise judgment. Due consideration must be given to the needs of others, but without sacrificing the educational welfare of the child. One good solution is to pick the child up and quickly move to a more secluded spot; this, however, may not always be practical or possible. In this case, try hard not to feel embarrassed as you wait out, without appeasing, the child's tantrum. A simple explanation can be offered to any disapproving or annoyed onlookers — for example, "I'm really sorry that her crying is annoying you, but she needs to learn that she can't have everything she wants."

When your child carries on at home in the presence of guests, it is usually best to take him immediately to another room and talk to him there.

## Guilt Feelings

Some parents automatically blame themselves whenever anything unpleasant happens. When there is conflict with their child, they assume it is they who are in the wrong. For example, a child is upset because he was denied permission to stay up late. The parent now begins to feel guilty. "I was mean, I made him feel bad, I should have let him stay up." The classic accusation "It's not fair!" triggers similar feelings. Children subconsciously sense their parents' doubts and learn to emphasize their hurt feelings even more in order to get their own way.

Parents need to stop such non-productive self-criticism and remind themselves that they are remaining firm for the benefit of the child.

Part of the problem of our guilt is our distress over causing another individual pain or suffering through our action. Certainly, this is praiseworthy. However, as parents we have a special obligation to educate our children.[7]

We must not forget that the commandment to avoid causing injury to others applies only to unnecessary injury. We must not hesitate to restrict our children when it is necessary for their benefit, even if we cause them anguish by doing so. Remember, the child's true suffering results from his unwillingness to tolerate frustration. We might well sympathize with him over his plight ("David, I know you'd like to stay up"), but we need not let his suffering influence us to change our minds ("but you still have to go to bed now").

Neither do we need to take the child's accusations of "It's not fair!" so seriously. While we might like to be perfectly fair, it is not always possible. If we demand it of ourselves, we are likely to instill similar demands for fairness in our child. But children must learn to endure some injustice as necessary preparation for life, and we had best cease striving for such unrealistic perfection.

At times, however, a parent may have valid second thoughts about the position he is taking. What should he do? It is best, in general, to stick to the original decision. Still, this does not have to be a hard-and-fast rule. If we occasionally regret a particular decision, we can certainly choose to reverse it or decide to handle the situation differently in the future. Of course, the reversal of a decision should not immediately follow the child's complaining, as that would only reinforce unpleasant behavior.

## AM I BEING SELFISH?

Sometimes parents feel guilty about asking their child to do things for them. They may, for instance, wish to ask the child to wash the dishes, but then hesitate. "Is it all right for me to make this request? Perhaps I'm being selfish. My child has a lot of homework (wants to play). Maybe I should be more considerate." They may also hesitate when they find it necessary to limit the child for reasons of convenience or economy.

Parents with this problem seem to believe that their needs must *always* be secondary to their child's needs. They mistakenly think they are selfish if they don't always give the child's desires precedence.

A hesitant manner subtly conveys to the child our inner anxiety. When you are unsure of your position, you can hardly expect enthusiastic cooperation. If you doubt your judgment, the child may also come to question it. Thus, without being aware of it, you may actually be encouraging self-centeredness in the child.

Moreover, parents who believe that they must put their child first *at all times* are harming both themselves and their child. After all, we all have limited reserves, and an exhausted parent cannot be an effective parent. Besides, constantly giving the child top priority in this way may easily lead to feelings of resentment toward him. Such feelings are bound to manifest themselves eventually in excess criticism and other aggressive behavior toward the child.

When parents feel guilty about burdening a child by requesting assistance in the home, they should keep in mind that providing him with opportunities to be helpful benefits him, too. As parents feel less guilty about such demands and more confident that they constitute good training for the child, it will become much easier to act firmly.

Guilt feelings may also push parents into doing things for their children when they are not really up to it. For example, the child may ask us to read him a story when we need to relax. If we tell ourselves "Come on, be nice — read him the story" and force ourselves to do it, the child probably senses that we are not really very happy about it, and derives no real pleasure from our sacrifice. There is nothing wrong in this case with giving preference to our own needs and telling the child pleasantly, "Sorry, honey, no story right now. I'm not really up to it."

## AM I EXPECTING TOO MUCH?

Lack of firmness sometimes results from unsureness about expectations. For instance, a small child will refuse to pick up his toys. The parent then hesitates, thinking, "Maybe we're expecting too much. The child is so young; I shouldn't be so strict." It is important to decide what we expect and to stick to it.

We may at times decide to raise or lower our expectations as we reassess our child's capacities. This must be done carefully and thoughtfully. It is counterproductive to impulsively change your expectations in the middle of an interchange with the child.

It is important not to be too concerned about your expectations. Even if you do at times expect too much of a child, you need not worry that this does real harm. Remember, you are bound to make mistakes. Forget about being perfect and just focus on trying to do your best.

## Fear of Disapproval and Rejection

Another reason some parents do not act firmly toward their children is that they fear displeasing them. These parents make the basic mistake of linking their worth to approval of others — in this case their child. Thus they are overly sensitive to any suggestion of criticism on his part, incorrectly interpreting disapproval to mean that they are not good parents.

If we are to manage our children effectively, we must stop connecting our worth to their approval. If our child disapproves of us, this is unfortunate. Even if there is warrant for his feelings, he is at best wrongly confusing us with our actions. We will feel less worthy only if we also forget to distinguish between ourselves and our behavior.

However, the child may not be judging us at all; he may simply be unhappy. It is our habit of judging ourselves negatively which leads us to conclude that our child is doing the same. Seeing ourselves in a negative light can seriously distort our perceptions.

Besides, it is unreasonable to expect that our children will always approve of our decisions. Some of us seem to believe that if we try hard enough, care enough, and sacrifice enough, we will win our child's constant approval. This is highly unrealistic. Some of our decisions are bound to disappoint the child, and he may, at such times, show his unhappiness or disapproval. As long as we have acted in our children's best interest, we should not allow their temporary displeasure to disturb us.

Perhaps our deepest fear about displeasing our children is that they will stop loving us. The parent who worries about losing a child's love may be afraid to deny him anything. The child, in turn, learns that everything will always go his way and becomes a small tyrant. If our motivation is "pleasing the child," we might very well end up with a not-so-pleasing child!

A small child who is angry at his mother for limiting him will sometimes react with insults such as "I don't like you," "You're not my friend," "Silly Mommy." Instead of taking such remarks seriously, we should view them as a natural manifestation of the child's immaturity. Parents should use their judgment in deciding whether to ignore such statements or perhaps answer softly, "I know you don't really mean that, but you're not allowed to say such things to Mommy."

## The Trap of Giving Reasons

Most parents are aware that children accept decisions more easily when they understand the reasons behind them. By giving the child explanations in this way, parents also provide the child a model of reasonableness.

Rabbi Hirsch writes that parents should give reasons for demands and restrictions so that the child not come to regard them as autocratic. However, a child should obey because he submits to his parents' better judgment, and not because their reasons appeal to him.[8]

Sometimes, parents feel compelled to justify a request because they fear that otherwise the child might not co-operate. The child, sensing that logic has become the deciding factor, will eagerly begin arguing. He rejects the first reason given; the parents now fall into the trap of offering more reasons — only to have the child reject them, too, one after another. The result is much unpleasant arguing. The child may even reject all the explanations offered and refuse to accept the decision altogether.

Giving reasons no longer serves a useful purpose if the child has come to demand them and believes that his obedience is contingent on his approval of them. In such a case, asking "Why" becomes a challenge rather than a legitimate request for a reason. It can also be a complaint — "Why do I have to do it?" At times, asking "Why" can even develop into a habit of arguing for argument's sake.

In order to discourage these unpleasant habits it is best to give the child one reason and one only. If it is rejected with an argument, remain firm. Have confidence in your ability to make your decisions stick. Offer no additional reasons, as these only provide the child with new opportunities to counterargue. Be persistent. If the child was asked to do something, insist pleasantly but firmly that he do as he was asked, and be prepared to continue to do so until he complies. Stay calm, pleasant, and non-judgmental. When his arguments bring the child no satisfaction, he may soon learn to stop them.

Here is an illustration:

> Child: I need five dollars spending money for the class trip tomorrow.
>
> Father: That's a little too much. We'll give you three dollars.
>
> Child: But all the other kids get five.
>
> Father: (Notice he does *not* offer another reason, such as "We can't afford it") Sorry — three is all you can have.
>
> Child: But I can hardly buy anything with three dollars!
>
> Father: I'm sorry but it will have to do.
>
> Child: Please, can't I have five?
>
> Father: No, three is all you can have.
>
> Child: It's not fair!
>
> Father: I'm sorry but you can't have more.

If your child continues to argue the first few times you use this approach, be patient. The fact that you responded or yielded to his arguments in the past has probably reinforced the arguing habit. If you want to start changing the situation now, you will have to resist some unpleasant arguing for a while.

While we should do our best to control feelings of annoyance toward the child for his arguing, there is nothing wrong with letting him know on occasion that we find it disagreeable. We might tell him, "It's not pleasant when you argue."

Our expectations have a way of being realized. Parents should try to develop an attitude which conveys to the child, in a friendly manner, "I expect you to accept my decisions even when you don't like my reasons."

One mother explained how she learned not to get sucked into endless arguments.

> There used to be a lot of arguing in our house — looking back on it. I feel it was because I either didn't sound convincing enough, or else I lost my temper at the first "No" and immediately yelled. Then I learned about avoiding arguments by giving one reason only, and continuing to be firm but calm even if that reason was rejected. After that, I felt emotionally ready for the next argument.
>
> The next day my five-year-old daughter wanted to change her everyday dress for a Shabbath dress. I said no, as there was no time to wash it before Shabbath. She insisted. I firmly repeated myself, "Rachel, you may not change your dress." I remained friendly but firm, as she continued to argue. Rachel finally gave up and *cheerfully* went off to play — no tears and recriminations. I guess she heard the determination in my voice.

Parents who are afraid that the child might not accept their real reason for a decision might be tempted to make up more palatable reasons. This bending of reality is good neither for the parent nor the child. Moreover, if these reasons are not completely honest, the child is likely to recognize them as mere excuses and try to argue them down. Therefore, it is best to stick to the real reason and completely ignore the child's reaction. For example, if a request for candy is being turned down, it is better for the parent to give his true reason — that it isn't good for the child to have too many sweets — than to offer the excuse, "It's too close to suppertime."

Rules such as "Ice cream only on Shabbath" or "Rooms have to be tidied up before supper" can be very helpful in eliminating the need for giving reasons, and can make it easier for the child to accept limits. At the time when the rule is established, the reason for it may be given. Thereafter, a friendly reminder is sufficient: "You know the rule about tidying up rooms."

In some situations it is not possible nor even desirable to give a reason at all. If the child has been taught to be obedient and accept the parents' better judgment, they should have no difficulty in enforcing their decision even when no reason is given. It should be sufficient to say, in a calm and pleasant manner, "I'm sorry, but I can't give you a reason now."

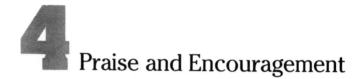

# 4 Praise and Encouragement

Two of the most powerful resources parents have for educating their children are praise and encouragement. The late Telzer Rosh Yeshivah, Rabbi Chaim Mordechai Katz, said that appreciative words help a person realize his own inherent worth and encourage him to utilize his attributes to the best of his ability.[1] Encouragement, praise, and appreciation bring out the best in a child, instilling a sense of security and confidence.

## Teaching Through Praise and Encouragement

Children have an innate need for affection and approval. They have a natural desire to please us, because this brings them, in return, expressions of love and praise. It is therefore important for us to let our children know what pleases us, by praising and encouraging their good behavior.

Children need to be told things like:

"You fixed breakfast for all of us. That's grownup behavior."

"Nice the way you got to bed on time this evening."

"I can really rely on you to take care of your little sister while I rest."

Praise in front of another important person can be especially rewarding. For example, the mother can announce to her husband in the evening, in the child's presence, "Daddy, I want you to know that Avi got dressed like a big boy today." The mother can enhance the effect of this praise if she tells the child in the morning, "When Daddy comes home, I'll tell him how well you dressed yourself today."

There is a certain amount of effort involved in keeping an eye open for agreeable behavior. It is much easier to notice what children do that disturbs us. The children may be playing quietly in their room, and we take no notice of it. But if they begin to be noisy, we are likely to go in and ask for quiet. It's much harder to remember to go in to commend them for their quiet and pleasant behavior while they are playing peaceably.

Try to be alert for improvements in a child's behavior and comment on them.

> "I hardly had to remind you this week to hang up your jacket."
>
> "I notice you're forgetting less often to bring your dishes to the sink."
>
> "You've improved in your table manners."

Opportunities for praise can sometimes be created.

> Mother (at the breakfast table): Aaron, let's see how carefully you can pour your milk this time so nothing spills.
>
> (Aaron pours carefully and succeeds)
>
> Mother: You were really careful. Nothing spilled at all.

Commend children for effort, too.

> "I notice you're making a real effort to get along better with your sister."

It takes practice. If a parent is not alert for opportunities to give praise, they will slip by unnoticed. But once the habit of expressing appreciation is established, it can bring about big changes in the children and in the atmosphere of the home.

## How to Praise

To be most effective, praise should be specific, appropriate, and objective.

### BEING SPECIFIC

When you praise, describe the behavior you liked. Avoid global praise such as "You're a wonderful boy" or "You're a very good girl." The intention of praise is to let the child know what specific aspects of his behavior are appreciated, so that he can continue them. That means focusing on what the child is doing.

If praise consists of general evaluations of the child, he may get the impression that his inherent worth is measured by his actions and accomplishments; or that your love for him depends on his behavior. Restricting praise to specific behavior will prevent these misconceptions.

### AVOIDING EXCESSIVE OR INAPPROPRIATE PRAISE

Although children benefit from frequent praise and appreciation, excessive or overly frequent praise is counterproductive. It may lead the child to depend on constant approval and recognition. The idea is to teach a child to appreciate himself, and not to teach him to rely on a steady supply of approval from others to maintain his self-esteem.

Excessive or inappropriate praise may also be rejected by the child, who senses that he does not really deserve it (for example, yesterday he hit his sister, so he knows he's not a shining example of perfection).

## OBJECTIVITY

It is important that our praise emphasize the value in the child's good behavior, and not merely our personal pleasure. For example, as you help the child put his toys away you might say, "The room looks nice when all the toys are put away" or "Isn't it nice when everything is in its place? Then we can find what we're looking for." The aim is to train the child to be conscious of an objective good, rather than of simply having pleased others. The ultimate goal is for the child to become an adult motivated solely by the desire to do God's will. With this in mind, parents can begin to encourage more abstract values such as mitzvoth and good character traits.

> "You did a real mitzvah when you helped that lady with her packages."
> "You washed the dishes even though you didn't feel well — that's showing *mesiruth nefesh* (self-sacrifice)."
> "You showed real self-control by not hitting your brother back."

This type of praise is incorporated in the custom of acknowledging good deeds with a blessing, *"yasher kochakha"* (more strength to you).[2]

## Encouraging Achievement

Encouragement gives children the self-esteem and enthusiasm needed to develop new skills. When we encourage our children, it is good to keep in mind that success at any particular task should not be our concern so much as instilling self-confidence in the child.

There are several aspects to encouraging achievement in children.

1. Giving help. When parents introduce a new skill, they must model how the task is done, explaining all the steps. But after the child understands the process, we need to withdraw a

bit and allow him the opportunity to work things out by himself. At the same time, we should be prepared to offer our help when it is needed.

When a child runs into difficulty in some task, parents frequently encourage him with "Come on, you can do it" or "It's not so hard." While this can be helpful, it may often be more encouraging to the child when we first show some empathy: "I see this is difficult for you" or "I see you're having a hard time." The child can then be encouraged to keep trying. We might also remind him, *"Kol hathchaloth kashoth"* (all things are difficult in the beginning).[3]

Often, a simple suggestion is all the child needs to help him over some difficulty. For example: "If you hold the sock the other way, it goes on more easily."

2. Expressing confidence. Encouragement can be as simple as a show of confidence in the child's judgment. Allow children to join family discussions and give them credit for the good ideas they contribute.

Also, try to avoid unnecessary cautions when children are working or playing: "Watch out, you'll fall!" "Be careful, that's going to break!" Even when it is necessary to caution a child, it can be done tactfully, such as, "Better not to make the cup so full."

3. Giving constructive criticism. When helping children improve their work, avoid merely pointing out what is wrong. Offer constructive suggestions and alternatives. For example, if a child has done a sloppy job on his arithmetic homework, say, "If you wrote those examples more clearly, they would be easier to read" rather than "It's impossible to read this!" You might also point to the most legibly written example commenting, "This one is a pleasure to look at. Maybe you could write all the others just as neatly."

4. Avoiding comparisons and competition. There are distinct individual differences among children. These must be taken into account. Allow each child to move at his particular pace without being compared to others.

5. Encouraging through praise. Make it a point, from time to time, to find some positive things to say about a child's work. For example:

> "Nice lettering on that sign."
> "What pretty colors in that painting."
> "That's some job on those candlesticks — they really sparkle!"

## Pride and Fear of Failure

Parents need to encourage and praise their children's accomplishments to help them develop self-confidence. However, as children learn to value their achievements, they need to be protected from two pitfalls: pride, and fear of failure.

Parents can protect children from pride by teaching them to be thankful for any abilities and talents with which they have been blessed. Children can also be taught to be modest about their accomplishments. The Sages teach, "If you have learned much, don't think highly of yourself for it, since for this you were created."[4] Parents can model modesty by reacting with gratitude, rather than pride, over their children's achievements, and by resisting the temptation to talk to others (especially in front of the children) about their children's cleverness and special attainments.

To protect a child against fear of failure, parents need to teach him that his personal worth is not measured by his accomplishments. While it is certainly desirable to do well, it does not make us better people. Our sages have taught that a person is required only to do his best. Whether he succeeds or not is not up to him.[5]

Parents should be careful not to pressure the child, or allow him to pressure himself, by insisting that everything he does must be perfect. They can also teach the child that mistakes are the way people learn, rather than signs of personal failure or reasons to rebuke ourselves.

## Rewards as a Method
## of Praise and Encouragement

Should rewards be used as incentives to encourage proper behavior in children? There are sharp differences of opinion on this question.

The view to be given here is that, while it is certainly best to rely on praise and other verbal reinforcement to influence children to behave well, rewards do have their place. They do motivate children and encourage them. However, they should be used only to get children to conform to basic behavioral requirements, such as keeping a neat room or getting to bed on time. They should not be used to induce children to do household chores, such as washing the dishes or taking the garbage out (see Chapter 7, "Reluctance to Help").

Some people question the use of rewards or prizes to encourage good behavior because they think it is a form of bribery. This is a mistake. A bribe, properly defined, is a prize or inducement offered someone in order to pervert his judgment or corrupt his conduct. A reward can be called a bribe only if our intention is to pervert or corrupt.

Another objection to rewards as incentives is that they accustom the child to always expect rewards for good behavior. The assumption here — that the child will continue to perform good deeds for inferior motives — is a false one. The Gemarah teaches, "A person should always fulfill Torah and mitzvoth even if he does so for ulterior motives because he will eventually come to do them for their own sake."[6]

We should never lose sight of the ideal. As our sages describe it, "Do not be like servants who serve their master for the sake of receiving a reward, but be rather like servants who serve their master without the intention of receiving a reward."[7]

Ultimately, good behavior will bring its own rewards. But children, who may not yet have experienced that intrinsic satisfaction which good behavior brings, may need our help in getting such behavior started. Rewards are simply a way to *initiate* a child into better behavior.

Rewards, of course, need not necessarily mean material rewards. A trip to a favorite spot can be a reward; so can the privilege to stay up late, or even to bake a cake. Whatever a child finds enjoyable can be used as reinforcement. Being allowed to play with some special toy or game can work well. By observing what a child normally enjoys doing, we can pick reinforcers that will be effective for him.

Incentives, however, tend to lose their effectiveness if parents keep reminding the child about them. They will then be seen by the child as just another form of pressure to get him to behave as we want. Parents have to be careful to keep themselves emotionally detached from the situation.

The point system is popular with many parents. The child is told which behavior he will be rewarded for; a chart for accumulation of points is posted in a conspicuous spot. When a certain amount of points have been accumulated, the child can trade these in for some prize — anything from a book or small toy to a mechanical pencil. Allow the child to choose the item he wishes. Prizes can be purchased and shown to the child beforehand. The reward can be non-material as well.

Star charts can be very reinforcing for young children. A star (let the child pick the color) is glued on every time, for instance, the child makes his bed. No other reward is necessary.

As an example of an innovative reinforcement system, suppose you want to teach your children not to leave their belongings scattered all over their room. Each child is given a small sum in the morning; but for every item found lying carelessly on the floor by evening (clothing, books, etc.) the child must give up a certain amount. Alternately, to prevent arguing, parents might decide to keep the money for the child and give it to him in the evening, minus whatever is forfeited.

## DRAWBACKS TO REWARDS

There are some serious drawbacks to using rewards. While

they may initially produce good results, they tend to lose their effectiveness with time. Also, sooner or later rewards must be discontinued. There is then the danger that the child will fall back into his old behavior patterns.

To mitigate these shortcomings, rewards should be gradually discontinued when the new habits have been firmly established. For example, if the child has been getting something special in his lunchbox for making his bed, the mother can say, "I don't think you need treats for making your bed anymore. But I'll give you a surprise in your lunchbox sometimes anyway."

## REWARDS FOR TORAH STUDY

Traditionally, rewards have always been given to children to encourage the study of Torah. The Talmud relates the story of an elementary school teacher who merited that his prayers for the community were answered immediately. When queried by the great sage Rav, he answered as follows:

> I teach young children. . . . And I have a pool of fish, and whoever does not wish to learn, I coax him with fish, and I entice and appease him, until he comes to learn.[8]

Rambam suggests that teachers encourage the young child to learn with things he loves, such as nuts or figs or a bit of honey.[9] Rabbi Yoel Schwartz writes:

> We may properly encourage better Torah learning through incentive rewards, for Torah studies are particularly difficult, and eventually, the child will feel the joy of learning without artificial inducements.[10]

In one home the children could choose a colorful postage stamp from their father's collection every time they came to study Torah. The father also kept in his desk drawer several beautifully illustrated animal books, as well as scientific equipment such as a magnifying glass and a magnet, for the children to amuse themselves with after the lesson.

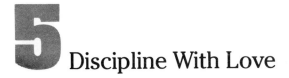

# Discipline With Love

There is a tendency to view discipline as a withholding of love. According to the Jewish view, however, not only is discipline an expression of true love, but withholding it from the child is actually a sign of hatred. "For he whom the Lord loves, He admonishes."[1] "Who spares his rod, [it is as if] he hates his child."[2] (Here we interpret "the rod" in its broadest sense, to include all forms of discipline.)[3] The disciplined child is also a source of true gratification to his parents. "Discipline your child, and he will grant you repose; he will give delight to your soul."[4]

The newborn baby is compared to a little wild donkey;[5] he follows only his natural instincts and primitive desires. Discipline is necessary to instill in the child those basic controls which will enable him to gradually acquire a less self-centered orientation.

## The Right Hand and the Left

In educating the child, the Sages advise, "Let the left hand push away while the right hand draws near."[6] We may see the right hand as symbolizing the *direct* expression of love — affection and understanding — and the left as representing the *indirect* expression of love, which appears as restriction and discipline. Rabbi Samson Raphael Hirsch explains that, while we combine love with strictness in our education, the "right hand drawing near" must predominate. "We cannot succeed in our education with excessive strictness, which only incites to rebelliousness." Only by expressing our constant love for the child can we succeed in educating him.[7]

While excessive severity is counterproductive and may lead to rebellion, the withholding of discipline is clearly no less harmful. Parents sometimes fail to discipline their child because of inappropriate feelings of compassion for him, or because they worry about interfering with his natural development. They are making a basic mistake. Perhaps the most tragic story in Scripture is that of Absalom's rebellion against his indulgent father, his violation of his father's wives, and his murderous drive to destroy his father. What could cause such perversion of human nature? The Midrash explains that the parent who deprives his child of discipline will cause him to follow evil ways and, eventually, to hate the parent. Because King David did not chastise or discipline his beloved son, Absalom became depraved, and even wanted to kill his father.[8] The absence of firmness and the unwillingness to discipline children can be basic causes for later rebellion against parents.

Note that the Sages refer to the withholding of discipline as *deprivation*. Discipline is necessary for the child; he has a right to it!

The strict left hand and the compassionate right hand may also be viewed as working together in another sense. When imposing discipline, we should do so in an obviously loving manner; this makes the child feel that we have his best interests in mind. Discipline which carries a message of love can never be interpreted by the child as rejection.

Modern psychology, too, recognizes the importance of discipline:

Much has been written about the dangers of harsh, oppressive, unloving discipline; these warnings are valid and should be heeded. However, the consequences of excessive punishment have been cited as justification for the elimination of discipline. That is foolish. . . . [The child] wants to know where the boundaries lie and who's available to enforce them . . . [and the parents] need to know when to punish, how to set limits, and what behavior to inhibit. This disciplinary activity must occur within the framework of love and affection.[9]

## Admonishment

The Torah commands us to admonish our fellow man when we see him behave improperly, as an expression of our love and concern for his welfare.[10] This mitzvah applies to our children with even greater force, for they are totally dependent on us for the development of their character and values.[11]

The Proverbs verse "For he whom the Lord loves, He admonishes" concludes with the words, "Like a father who delights in his son." The Gaon of Vilna comments that the father-son relationship is unlike other relationships where, even though the rebuker loves the one whom he rebukes, he eventually lets him go his way if he does not listen. But if the son does not heed the father's rebuke, the father does not desist but continues to chastise him until the son improves his ways. He does this out of a love which is so great that it cannot bear to see wrongdoing, and desires only that the son behave righteously. The evidence that the father acts out of feelings of love is that when he is finished chastising his son, he speaks to him comfortingly and soothingly. When the admonishment is followed by comforting words, it is unlikely to cause resentment, for the child will sense that it is really an expression of love.

## PRINCIPLES OF ADMONISHMENT

*Purpose.* When admonishing their child, parents should clearly convey to him that they act out of concern for his welfare. As the Rambam says: "Speak pleasantly and softly when you admonish someone. Explain to the person that you have only his benefit in mind, to bring him to eternal life in the world to come."[12]

*Timing.* While we should not hesitate to admonish our children, there is a special obligation of "not saying that which will not be heeded."[13] This means that it may sometimes be necessary to postpone the admonishment until the child is most receptive to being rebuked. (A child's wrongdoing must never, of course, be entirely overlooked, for he may then interpret our silence as approval.) Thus, with the exception of very young children, it is often better not to admonish the child on the spot, but rather to wait for an opportune moment. This may be an hour or so later, sometimes even a day or two. It is important that both the parent and the child be calm enough for a serious and friendly conversation about the behavior. It is said of Rabbi Eliyahu Lopian that before reprimanding any of his children or students, he would always allow enough time to elapse so that not a trace of anger remained. Once when one of his children did something extremely improper, he waited two full weeks until he censured him.[14]

Parents must also be careful not to admonish the child in front of others, lest they cause him embarrassment or shame.[15] (The prohibition against causing embarrassment or shame extends to private admonishments as well.)[16]

*Avoiding anger.* When admonishing a child, our goal is to influence him to regret his behavior and work to change it. This cannot be accomplished with angry rebukes. Anger should be reserved for those rare occasions when we need to forcefully impress a child with the gravity of his wrongdoing.

Even then, we only act as if we are angry; inwardly we remain calm.[17]

*Positive expectations.* When Aaron the priest met a wrong-doer, he would greet him in a friendly manner. When the transgressor was tempted the next day to do wrong again, he would think, "How will I face Aaron, who greeted me as if he considers me righteous? I feel ashamed to do wrong."[18]

When admonishing a child, one should convey that one expects the best of him. In the words of the Ran:

> Anyone wishing to correct a person who has done wrong, should do this in two ways. First he must let him know that he did wrong . . . second, let him know that he is capable of reaching a high level [of perfection] — that despite his wrongdoing he is beloved by his friend and remains in his good graces.[19]

The Shelah teaches us that if we tell someone, when admonishing him, that such conduct does not befit so intelligent and wise a person as he, he will feel complimented and more receptive to correction.[20]

If we are to influence our children, they must sense our belief in their ability to change. They must never get the impression that we have given up on them.

When parents view their child's negative traits as fixed, they inevitably convey this by such statements as:

> "Batya can't do what I ask without giving me an argument."
> "Dinah makes a fuss about every little thing — she's such a complainer."
> "Nothing remains in one piece after Benjamin is finished with it."
> "Pinchas can't make up his mind about anything."

The labels parents commonly give their children, such as "irresponsible," "lazy," or "stubborn," have the same effect. "Labeling is disabling," writes a noted child psychologist.[21] Rabbi Hirsch states: "If we give up hope concerning our children, and fail to muster the energy to guide them onto the proper path, they too will give up hope concerning themselves."[22]

## MANNER OF ADMONISHMENT

People don't like to be told that they are wrong. Children are no exception, and should be admonished, writes the Gaon of Vilna, with "soft words and reprimands which will be willingly accepted."[23]

Our admonishment can consist of a few words delivered on the spot, or it can take the form of a serious discussion with the child. *What* we say is not quite as important as *how* we say it. If we are calm inside and feel loving concern for the child, then the words we choose will usually be the right ones.

Consider the following rebuke: "When I called you before, you ignored me and continued playing. Is that right? What are you supposed to do when I call you?" Imagine this being said in an attacking and accusatory tone of voice, and picture the effect on the child. Now think of the same words said gently, and imagine their very different effect.

We should be aware to what extent our tone of voice, even the expression on our face, can convey a "putdown" message, often far more effectively than our words. Watch yourself in a mirror as you say, "You shouldn't have done that" in three different ways: first angrily; then with mild annoyance; then lovingly. The child is no less aware of the contrast!

Keep in mind that a deep sigh, a look of disgust, or even pursed lips can convey our negative thoughts about the child. Children are masters at studying our faces for signals of disapproval, and we should do all we can to control such negative signals — and, ultimately, the negative thoughts behind them.

Admonishing a child with "Why did you . . ." or "Why didn't you . . ." is generally ineffective and should be avoided. These types of rebukes are really criticisms of the child and, unless said extremely gently are unlikely to motivate him to improve his behavior. For example, your daughter has come home from school with her dress full of glue stains. You know that the stains won't come out and that the dress is ruined. You reprimand her, "Why weren't you more careful?" This statement really conveys, "You *should have* been more careful." It implies a negative judgment of the child. She will react either by defensively warding off your criticism, or by accepting it and feeling down about herself ("Mommy's right — I don't know why I'm so careless!"). In either case, she is unlikely to be thinking constructively about how she might avoid staining her clothing in the future. A better approach, more likely to succeed would be to tell the child, "You know, those glue stains don't come out. This dress can't be worn anymore. You've got to be more careful when you work with glue." Of course, the way we say this makes all the difference.

Reprimanding the child by repeating back to him a description of his negative behavior is another pattern to avoid. A lively five-year-old thinks it delightful fun to use the sofa as a trampoline. Mother cries out, "You're ruining my furniture!" But these words don't convey mother's understandable concern about the sofa. What they mainly convey is her annoyance over the child's behavior. Consequently, he feels put down and possibly even resentful. A better reaction would be, "Honey, please stop. The furniture gets ruined when you jump on it like that."

When correcting a child, remember to state your expectations clearly. It does little good to complain to a child, "Why do you always run out in the middle and leave me with the rest of the cleaning up to do by myself?" Instead, we should call him in and tell him, "I'd like you to stay in the kitchen after supper to help me until everything is cleaned up."

It is good to sit down with the child during your talk with him. You might want to reassure him of your love by taking his hand in yours, or putting your hand on his shoulder. Try whenever appropriate to begin with something favorable. Here are some examples:

"I guess you probably forgot . . ."
"Perhaps you weren't aware . . ."
"I know you were in a hurry before and that's why . . ."
"I realize it was hard for you to control yourself . . ."
"I'm sure you didn't intend to . . ."

Don't corner the child. Give him a chance to explain things from his point of view. Don't knock his reasons down or label them excuses. You can show understanding at the same time that you point out what was wrong with his behavior. Often, a simple reminder such as "Remember what we said about . . . ?" is all that is needed. Try to end the session on an optimistic note, conveying confidence in the child's desire to improve his behavior.

Sometimes merely telling the child "I'm disappointed in you" can be sufficient admonishment. Or one can say, "I guess I don't have to tell you that you acted wrongly before — you probably realize it yourself, don't you?"

Even a disappointed look alone, which lets the child know "I expect better of you," can at times suffice. Parents must let the child's nature guide them in deciding what forms of reprimand will work best. For some very sensitive children the mildest of rebukes is enough.

One mother tells of the effect on her child when she changed to a quiet manner of admonishing:

My two boys had had a fight. Eli, seven and a half, had torn a picture which his younger brother of five brought home from school. Normally I would have scolded him in a loud voice, "Eli, you shouldn't have done that — it wasn't very nice! How would you like it if someone did that to you?" His reaction would then have been defensive, something like, "He started it!" and so on, ending up in a very unpleasant argument.

This time I waited until evening. I called Eli in and told him quietly, "I want to speak to you." I had him sit down next to me and, taking hold of his hand, told him in a serious but quiet voice, "Eli, what you did this afternoon wasn't so nice — it wasn't right — you shouldn't have done it. . . ." At that point he burst into tears. I was so surprised. With a few quiet words, I got through to him so easily.

It is important that parents not become overly cautious, worrying about every word they say. Although we should make reasonable efforts to avoid hurting the child, sharp words will sometimes be necessary. Indeed, if parents are too careful to avoid any and all sharp words, the child may become overly sensitive to minor slights which others easily overlook.

## WHEN REPEATED ADMONISHMENT HAS NOT HELPED

It is no secret that staying calm is most difficult when our repeated admonishments have failed to affect the child. At these times we are likely to think to ourselves, "This is it. I've talked to him about this nicely time and again, but it doesn't seem to make any difference. Now I'm going to let him have it."

Parents should be aware, however, that if they allow themselves to get angry at this point, their efforts to stay calm until now have been largely wasted. We must remember that one of the main reasons the child does not improve his behavior is that he tells himself how bad he is for misbehaving, rather than making determined efforts to change. Our anger strongly reinforces this habit. However, parents should be careful not to repeat the child's mistake by telling *themselves* off for their inability to stay calm. Seeing our own difficulties in this respect may help us to be more tolerant of the child and show him more understanding.

In our talks with the child we must make special efforts to speak quietly. It is appropriate to ask questions which call for an explanation of his behavior, such as "How come you're still doing this when I've talked to you about it so many times?" When said gently, this is bound to evoke in the child genuine feelings of regret. Sometimes we might add, "I know you're sorry, but that's not enough. You have to make up your mind to act differently next time." One might also gently rebuke the child, "It's not right for you to keep ignoring my requests like this."

## REACTIONS TO ADMONISHMENT

Often, children will remain completely quiet when we talk to them. This does not mean that they are not listening to us. They may be taking in everything we say, while simply not feeling like answering. Give them time to think things over and don't rush them.

Some children will heavily defend themselves even when mildly admonished. This is because admonishment triggers in them uncomfortable guilt feelings, which they then try to ward off by a defensive reaction.

In dealing with defensive reactions, it is important to avoid trying to prove the child wrong. If his defense is a flimsy one, he is usually well aware of it and does not need it pointed out to him. For example, when asked why he neglected to do some chore, the child may answer with that best known of excuses, "I forgot." It is best to take him at his word and answer, "Please try harder to remember next time."

Parents should be aware to what extent their manner of rebuking their child until now may have contributed to his guilt problem and subsequent defensiveness, and be careful to avoid triggering guilt in the future. If we keep our remarks objective and avoid putdowns, the child will, in time, get over his guilt feelings and no longer feel compelled to defend himself.

Ideally, we may be able to instill in a child the ability to admit his mistake and express regret over it. Consider the following exchange:

> Mother: We've talked about not leaving your papers and books lying around the living room. This morning I found your things there again.
>
> Child: It was only a few papers.
>
> Mother (gently): Honey, you don't have to defend yourself. Just tell me, "I'm sorry, Mom, I'll try to remember for next time."

Angry or hostile reactions are also brought on by guilt feelings, except that in this case the child is blaming us for making him feel bad. Parents should never allow such reactions to put them on the defensive, and certainly not permit a child's angry outburst to deter them from admonishing him in the future. It is best to tell him, "I see you're very upset. I'll talk to you later when you've calmed down."

Later, when the child has regained his composure, you can say to him, "I realize you were feeling bad before and that's why you screamed at me. But you know that's wrong. If I tell you something which upsets you, you can tell me that you feel bad, but you're not allowed to yell." Try to get the child to see that you correct him because you care about him, and don't want him to do wrong things. You might say, "I know you're very unhappy right now. But please try to understand that when I correct you, it's because I care about you so much. I have only your best interest at heart."

Often, a child feels very bad after being admonished. He may even be telling himself off for his poor behavior. We can ease the child's guilt feelings by telling him, "I know you're sorry."

On the other hand, the child may act as if he isn't bothered at all by our rebuke. He may even say, "I don't care." We can respond by putting our hand on his shoulder and telling him, very lovingly, "I know you don't really mean that."

## Punishment

In general, parents should rely on admonishment to correct their children's behavior. However, when repeated reprimands have not worked, we may sometimes need to punish the child. Punishment should not be seen as a last resort, but as an occasionally necessary disciplinary tool. Like admonishment, it is a Torah obligation.[24]

Some parents hesitate to punish their child because they are reluctant to cause him suffering. It may help them to overcome this if they can regard punishment as a kind of bitter-tasting medicine which is sometimes the only cure for misbehavior.

Other parents hesitate to punish because they have been influenced by modern ideas about punishment which claim that it is an unfair use of power that leads to feelings of hatred and revenge in the child. This may be so when parents punish vengefully or in anger — but that, clearly, is not the Jewish way. Rabbi Shlomoh Wolbe writes:

> [Sometimes] when the child does not immediately obey, the father feels personally offended. He then "punishes" the child. In truth, this is not punishment but revenge, and revenge is forbidden by Torah law toward a child too.[25]

> The sensitive heart of the young child is strongly affected by every expression of pain on the part of his parents. And if we deprive him of part of his usual portion of sweets, this is already significant punishment; certainly so if he is deprived of all of it![26]

We learn from the Talmud that we should punish a child only after he has been forewarned and knows what to expect if he continues to misbehave.[27] Punishments should never be announced and then deferred; parents should either punish immediately or overlook the misdeed, since in anticipation of a punishment a child may be frightened to the point of harming himself.[28] Parents are also cautioned to be extremely sparing in punishing older children.[29]

The parents' manner at the time of punishment should convey to the child how badly they feel about having to administer it. They should always explain to the child why he is being punished.

## PHYSICAL PUNISHMENT

Physical punishment will be discussed first, not because it is the best method, but because it is so frequently used.

Normally, it is forbidden to strike others.[30] Nevertheless one is permitted to hit a child as punishment, but only to the extent that it is necessary for educating him.[31] It is, however, poor practice to rely on hitting as an educational tool.[32] The Talmudic sage Rav advises, "When you hit a child, do not hit him with anything but a shoe strap,"[33] to which Rashi comments, "In other words, a light stroke which can do no harm."

The Gaon of Vilna writes that a parent should not strike his child cruelly and out of anger for what he has done. Rather, the physical punishment should be intended to prevent the child from behaving badly in the future. Also, the parent should not hit the child more than a few times.[34] Moreover, Jewish law forbids administering physical punishment to a grown child.[35] This prohibition is based on the biblical injunction, "You shall not place a stumbling block before the blind."[36] That is, by striking a grown child, one may incite him to hit back and thereby violate a serious biblical injunction against striking a parent. Even hitting one's small child too frequently is wrong, and parents are liable to court sanctions for it.[37]

Modern psychologists have pointed out the harm done by

hitting children (some even advocate the elimination of *all* forms of punishment!), and many parents have become extremely reluctant to do so. Yet the various objections raised to hitting children — that it is harmful and cruel; that it causes the child to hate his parents; that it teaches him to be aggressive and cruel to others — need not concern us if we adhere to the above-mentioned limitations. When parents are careful to observe these restrictions, acting, when they hit their child, only out of concern for his welfare, hitting need not be either harmful or cruel. The child is unlikely to hate his parents for hitting him; nor is there any danger that he will learn from the parents' example to become aggressive and cruel to others.

The child should be impressed not so much by the pain of the slap as by the fact that it was *necessary* for the parent to hit him. To convey this idea, a serious, perhaps even somber mood should prevail at the spanking session. At the same time, we should remember that children are often very upset after being hit and in need of reassurance that we still love them. Therefore, it is a good idea to show them some affection not too long after the spanking.

The following incident reported by one mother illustrates how effective even a gentle slap on the hand can be:

> Our four-year-old was in the habit of calling everyone, including me, *"meshuga'at"* (crazy). I reprimanded her several times in a quiet tone of voice: "I can't allow you to call me that." She persisted in using the word. I tried ignoring her for a while, but this didn't seem to help either. I explained to her what the word means and how it hurts people's feelings to be called such a name, but this seemed to have little effect since she continued her behavior.
>
> In order to help myself control my anger and annoyance at my daughter, I reminded myself that the child was not bad, but rather that she had a bad habit,

and that it was my job to help her break it. These thoughts enabled me to remain calm and to attempt to deal effectively with the problem.

One day when the older children were out of the house, my daughter asked me for something that I was unable to give her at the moment. Her reaction was to call me *"meshuga'at."* I walked over to her, took her hand and said *quietly* to her, "I have asked you to stop calling me *meshuga'at*, but I see that you forget. I have to hit you now, to help you remind yourself." Then I hit her gently on her hand. She ran out of the room crying. She cried for a long time. Since then, she has not mentioned the word.

Slapping children routinely for all kinds of minor misbehavior is poor disciplinary practice. Keeping children in line by warning them, "You're going to get slapped if you do that!" is similarly ill advised. For hitting to be effective, it must be used very sparingly.

## OTHER KINDS OF PUNISHMENT

*Sending a child to his room.* This is an appropriate punishment for many kinds of minor misbehavior. For instance, the child may be wild and unruly. He can be told, very calmly, "Please go to your room now for a while. You can come out when you're ready to control yourself." The child may then, if necessary, be taken by the hand and led to his room (or some other room). If he comes out soon afterwards and resumes his wild behavior, we should tell him, "I see you're not yet ready to control yourself. Please go back to your room." Alternatively, the child can be asked to stay in the room for a specified amount of time. To prevent him from coming out to ask "Can I come out now?" you can put a timer in the room, explaining that he cannot come out until it rings.

Before sending the child out, it is advisable to warn him at least once: "Either you settle down or I'll have to send you to your room."

When a child refuses to go to his room or to stay in it, we may need to forewarn him of other punishment to follow if he does not obey us. In the above situation, for example, we might say very quietly, "You decide — you can go to your room or miss your applesauce for dessert tonight." We have to make our punishments stick. Even if the child acts as if he doesn't care, he will be sorry he didn't listen to us when he misses his dessert.

What about locking a child in the room? Many object to locking a child into a room because they believe it could traumatize him. Certainly, this is an extreme measure; however, there may be times when it is necessary. The child must be forewarned of the consequences — "You can either stay in the room or I'll have to lock it" — the choice is then his. Usually it is not necessary to repeat this action. Neither does the door have to be locked for long — we can unlock it as soon as the child agrees to stay in the room. One can also hold on firmly to the doorknob, letting the child know that we are ready to release it when he decides to remain in the room.

Children will sometimes begin to kick, bang, or throw objects when they are sent to their room. If there is danger of any damage, the behavior must be stopped immediately, either by physically restraining the child or by sending him out of the house. Naturally, we have to exercise good judgment as to whether sending him out may be risky if the child is too upset.

*Depriving a child of treats.* Be careful, when using this punishment, that it does not produce strong resentment. A reduction in the child's usual portion is recommended. Thus, he has his crackers at snacktime without the usual peanut butter; he gets only half a bag of potato chips or half a piece of cake for dessert.

*Deprivation of privileges.* One can punish a child by not allowing him to ride his bicycle for a day. For instance, if a child dawdles about getting to bed at night, we might deprive him of a day's bike riding for each fifteen minutes late to bed. If a child has come in late several times, or if he misbehaves while outside, an especially fitting punishment is that he be kept in the house. True, this may be hard on the mother, but it may be worth her while to go through one difficult day if this will produce a change in the child's behavior.

*Punishment for disrespect.* As discussed in Chapter 2, showing respect to them is one of a child's basic obligations to his parents. Occasional disrespect is best dealt with by gentle rebukes. However, when a child has been unusually disrespectful, punishment may sometimes be called for. One effective and suitable punishment is to refrain from speaking to him for, say, three hours. Since our purpose is to impress the child with the seriousness of his transgression, it is important to explain to him quietly beforehand that he is being punished. One might say, for example: "For the next three hours I am not talking to you. You shouted at me — that's no way to talk. This is your punishment." For a younger child half an hour is usually sufficient.

It must be made obvious that this punishment is not a form of retaliation but rather a measure deemed necessary for the child's welfare. Thus the parent, feeling no anger, calmly ignores the child for the specified time. He pays no attention to any complaining or carrying on about the punishment, just as he would ignore a child's resistance to swallowing a bitter-tasting medicine. Nothing need be said when the punishment is over; resumption of normal relations can begin immediately. Do not make remarks such as "I hope you learned your lesson." Like any other disciplinary action, however, this one loses its effectiveness if resorted to frequently.

## REACTIONS TO PUNISHMENT

Parents should not permit a child's reactions to punishment to affect them. To get back at their parents, children will sometimes sulk to show them how angry they are at being punished. If the parents ignore it, the child will see that he is only punishing himself and will stop. Other children project an "I don't care" attitude; this too should be ignored.

On the other hand, violent protest, whether directed against objects like chairs or the parents themselves, cannot be overlooked. For suggestions on how to cope with such behavior, see "Abusive Behavior" in Chapter 3.

## Natural and Logical Consequences*

Effective discipline sometimes requires that we refrain from interfering in the natural order of events, allowing children to experience the direct unpleasant results — that is, natural consequences — of their misbehavior. For example, clothes which are not put into the hamper don't get washed. When a child fails to get up on time he is inevitably late for school and must face the teacher's displeasure. Children who come in late for supper get a cold meal, or miss the meal altogether.

Logical consequences, by contrast, are the *arranging* of events so that unpleasant consequences follow. For instance, objects left lying around the house end up in a box kept in some out-of-the-way spot. A child who neglects to brush his teeth can't have dried fruit or other sweets because sticky foods, if not removed by brushing, can harm teeth. A child who misbehaves when the family is out visiting stays home the next time. The child should always be informed beforehand of negative consequences, so that he has a choice in the matter. Thus, the child who misbehaves on a visit is quietly told, "Either you behave nicely or we'll have to leave you home with a baby-sitter the next time we go visiting."

---

* These concepts were first formulated by Rudolf Dreikurs in *The Challenge of Parenthood* (New York: Duell, Sloan & Pearce, 1948).

# 6 Developing an Understanding Relationship

In elaborating on the mitzvah "Love your fellow as yourself,"[1] Rambam writes: "All the things you want others to do for you, do them to your brother in Torah and mitzvoth."[2] This principle has special implications for the way we nurture our children.

On the most basic level, of course, is the physical care we give them: our provision of a home, food, health. But we also give of ourselves emotionally — whether with a smile and a friendly word,[3] or, in a deeper way, by extending them empathy. Empathy means putting oneself in the other person's position, imagining what it's like from his point of view, and letting him know that we understand. It is valuable to all people, and certainly to growing children dependent on others for support and guidance. It is among the most lofty forms of *chesed* (lovingkindness), one of the cornerstones of Torah life[4] (see the next chapter).

In addition to empathy and understanding, children want to have their ideas and opinions respected. They can usually tolerate disagreement so long as they feel that their ideas are granted some legitimacy.

Children flourish best when we extend them this empathy, understanding, and respect.

## Learning to be More Empathic

We often quickly jump in and give advice when our children come to us with their problems. We tend to discount their feelings or tell them how they should feel. Instead, we should stop and ask ourselves, "How would I want someone else to respond to me if I were in the child's position?"

One good way to become more empathic is to keep in mind how dissatisfying an unempathic response can be when we ourselves want some understanding from another person. For example, imagine yourself a housewife with four little children. It is two weeks before Pesach and you have been working hard all day. When your husband comes home you greet him with a wan smile as you tell him, "I'm completely worn-out." He replies, "I keep telling you you're doing too much. Half the work you do is totally unnecessary." How do you feel? Not understood, and perhaps even upset. You would no doubt have liked to hear something like, "I can see you're completely exhausted. You must have really worked hard. Why don't you go rest a bit while I put the kids to sleep?" At another time you might be willing to listen to the well-intentioned advice of doing less unnecessary work, but not at this moment.

Becoming more empathic toward our children takes practice. Before we give advice, it is important to let the child know that we understand his position. We have to learn to curb that initial impulse to tell him what to do or how he should feel, instead first taking the time to really listen to him. Though it may require some effort, the results are well worth it, as these stories illustrate:

> When my children came to me with a problem in the past, I was not really listening to their problem. I generally didn't empathize with them. Often, I'd discount their problem entirely. Now I'm learning the values of listening more and empathizing with my

children. Of course, I forget sometimes and continue to tell them what to do or not to do and how they should feel (how I feel!). Usually I get nowhere with my sermonizing — the problem prolongs itself. But when I do remember to empathize, the problem usually resolves itself immediately.

For example, last week my son returned from his music lesson in tears and visibly upset. He sobbed, "Mommy, it's so hard. I can't learn to play melodica any more!" (The previous week I had asked the teacher to give him more songs for practice since I felt that the material was too easy for him.) In the past I would have said, "I think it's easy, so why are you sobbing and crying?" He would continue, "I can't do it anymore!" Then I would have said, "But it's easy, isn't it?" And so it would go on. This time I tried showing empathy. I said, "It must have been hard for you this evening." He answered, "Yeah." I suggested, "It really was a rough lesson, wasn't it?" All he said was "Yeah." He seemed to feel satisfied that I understood him and stopped complaining and sobbing. That's all there was to it.

We had an ongoing problem with our eleven year-old-son, who didn't want to go to his Pirchei group on Shabbath afternoon. Then he would complain endlessly, "I have nothing to do." A fifteen-minute argument would then ensue — "Yonathan, you have to go!" "Why should I go — we don't do anything anyway." "Just go — you'll have a good time." "No, I don't want to." "Yonathan!" (with the pitch of my voice raised an octave). Finally he would go out the door, with both of us feeling bad.

This time when he came to me saying, "I don't want to go today," I turned to him and said, "Yonathan, I know you don't like to go to the Pirchei, but it's so much better for you to go than to stay here and be bored."

He got up and walked out of the room. I was sure he was just going to read in his room, but in a minute I heard the front door open — he walked out and went to Pirchei.

## Creating an Atmosphere of Understanding

In creating an atmosphere of understanding, parents must be patient, empathic, and good listeners. However, there are several things they should watch out for.

1. Avoid contradicting or discounting the child's perceptions. Try to give legitimacy to his opinions. If he says, for example, "Yuch! This milk tastes sour!" don't tell him, "Why, you can hardly taste it." When he tells you that his drawing "didn't come out well," don't answer, "Well, I think it's nice." We tend to respond this way because we are trying to influence the child. In the first example, we are trying to persuade him to drink the milk. However, the predictable outcome here is an argument with each side maintaining his position. Far better to reflect back with, "The milk tastes sour to you?" The issue here is not whether the child must drink the milk or not, but one of showing respect for a legitimate opinion. The parent can suggest flavoring the milk to cover up the slightly sour taste. (If the child then still does not want to drink the milk, he should certainly not be forced to.)

In the second example, the parent wants to encourage the child to continue drawing. Here too, however, the child will most likely keep insisting that his drawing isn't good. An understanding response, one which confirms the child's point of view, might be, "You're dissatisfied with the way your drawing turned out." This, surprisingly, is often more encouraging to the child.

Parents should not try to get a child over any unhappiness

or despondency by telling him, for instance, "Never mind. You'll get over it" or "Come on, it's not so bad. Snap out of it." Children (adults as well!) don't like being talked out of their feelings. It is better to acknowledge the child's feelings with, for example, "How disappointing! You were so looking forward to that trip and now it was canceled because of the weather." Our empathy and understanding usually suffice to help children get over their unhappy feelings.

A further illustration: Your teen-age son has torn his pants while crawling under a fence. He is unhappy because he realizes that his carelessness will cost his parents a new pair of pants. Better not to console him with, "Never mind — we'll buy you new pants." He will feel better if we reflect his feelings. "You're unhappy because you're blaming yourself for your carelessness and you're thinking about how much money we'll have to spend for new pants."

In reflecting a child's feelings, however, parents must exercise certain cautions. For example, complaints about another person's behavior usually constitute forbidden derogatory speech, and we should gently point this out. If your child tells you he is angry at his friend, it would be wrong to answer, "Boy, you really felt like punching him in the nose, didn't you!" Anger is a bad character trait. While we do not condemn the child for his anger, we must not encourage his expressing it.

Remember that understanding a child's feelings does not mean we have to agree with them. Often it is a mistake to do this. For instance, in the above example of the canceled picnic, it would be foolish to say, "You're right. It really is terrible that the picnic was called off."

Keep in mind that sometimes children are totally unreceptive to empathy, preferring to be left alone. You can find out if the child wants to talk or would rather be left alone by asking, "I see you are upset. Do you want to talk about it?"

At times, children actually want to be talked out of their feelings of discouragement. One mother, whose fifteen-year-old son was worried about the possibility of an injury to his ankle becoming permanent, told us about the boy's reaction when she empathized with him by reflecting his feelings. "I don't want to hear that," he told her. "I want you to assure me that it's nothing serious." We need to sense what is appropriate in each situation.

2. Avoid challenging the child. Questions such as "Do you mean to tell me...?" or "Are you sure?" or "How do you know that?" put the child on the defensive. They convey a lack of trust in his judgment. Parents should refrain in general from "cross-examining" the child and asking too many probing questions.

3. Avoid imposing your opinions on the child. Don't get into arguments about who is right or whose ideas are better; this only results in polarization of positions. Try, whenever possible, to find something in the child's statements with which you can agree. Even when you don't agree with what a child says, you can still comment, "That's interesting," "I hadn't thought about it that way before," "That could be." Remarks such as "That's ridiculous" or "How could you say something so silly" or "You don't know what you're talking about" show disregard, both for the child's opinion and his feelings.

When we do express disagreement, it can be done pleasantly — "I don't quite agree with you," "I don't see it that way," "I have a different opinion." When the child suggests a way of doing something which we must reject, we can say, "I'm sorry but I can't accept that idea."

4. Give advice sparingly. As well-meaning as our advice may be, children want and need a chance to learn from their own experience. Too much interference with their affairs can lead ultimately to resentment and a general resistance to all advice. When we wisely reserve our advice for when it is really needed, it is far more likely to be accepted.

If your advice is rejected, don't argue. For example, a teen-age girl studies every evening late into the night. The parent advises, "I think it might be a good idea to study a little less and go to bed earlier. I'm worried that you're not getting enough sleep." She replies, "Don't worry, I can manage. I'm not tired." Further efforts to induce her to go to bed earlier are unlikely to succeed. If the parent nevertheless continues trying, she will only resist. It is best to end the discussion by conveying to her a confidence in her ability to make sensible decisions.

A good way to offer advice, when it was not specifically requested, is to ask straightforwardly, "Would you like some advice on this?" or "Would you like to hear what I would do in your situation?" This spares the child from having to ward off unsolicited advice, and spares us the unpleasantness of having our suggestions turned down.

Do your best to avoid getting into "yes, but" discussions, where you keep offering suggestions which the child turns down with a "yes, but" reply. If the child rejects your suggestions, respect his right to do so. Don't warn him of the dire consequences to follow. Don't show resentment or make deprecating remarks. Also, don't tell him in disgust, "Okay. Do whatever you want." Keep in mind that the child wants our approval of his ideas, and will try hard to win it by presenting reasons to support them. If we wish to influence the child to accept our point of view, we should first show that we understand his position, only then presenting our suggestions in a friendly way. For instance, we can say, "I understand what you're saying but I'm wondering if . . ." If the child remains uninfluenced, we can always end the discussion with, "All right — why don't you think about it a little?" Children do often reconsider our advice later, after they have had time to think things over and feel less threatened by loss of honor because of capitulation.

Children often learn by unpleasant experience that they would have been better off following their parents' advice. Parents should refrain from moralizing at such times. For instance, the family is about to leave on a long bus trip and you remind the children to go to the bathroom. One child insists that he doesn't have to go. An hour later, when you are on the bus, he suddenly tells you he does need the bathroom. Don't say, "Why didn't you go when I told you?" or "You see what happens when you don't listen to me?" Limit your words to, "I'm really sorry but you'll have to wait until we're off the bus." On future trips he is likely to follow your advice.

We should not always assume, when children come to discuss their problems, that they want help. Our advice may even sound to them like criticism because it implies they aren't handling the situation properly. Frequently, all the child wants is a sympathetic ear and a chance to get things off his chest or clarify his thinking. If we listen to him with an occasional "Hmm" or "I see" or "I know what you mean," he may well solve his problem all by himself. Some simple reflecting back also greatly facilitates the "unloading" process — for example:

> "You're having a hard time deciding whether you want to take piano or guitar lessons."
> "You're feeling discouraged about French."
> "With so much homework you're thinking you won't have any time to play."

Even when children ask for our advice, we need not always give it immediately. We can try sometimes to help them arrive at solutions on their own by asking, for example, "What do you think you could do?" If the child replies "I don't know," we can suggest, "Have you thought of . . . ?"

We may sometimes need to intervene to prevent an older child from making a major decision which could be unwise. For example, an older son wishes to enroll in a school which we think is not suitable for him. We can tell him, "This is a very serious decision. You may not have thought this through properly. Let's sit down and discuss the pros and cons." The parents may nevertheless elect to permit the boy to make his own decision; in this case they should let him know from the beginning that the final choice will be his.

Parents should never hesitate to tell their child that they think he is making a serious mistake. For example, if a teen-age child decides to spend a large sum of his own money on an item which you feel is not worth it, you can let him know how you feel. Children are often thankful to their parents later for their advice.

Being only human, parents will occasionally err in their judgment. When this happens they should not hesitate to tell their child, "I'm sorry, I made a mistake." Parents need not worry that appearing before their child as fallible will undermine their authority or the child's confidence in them; on the contrary, it builds up confidence. The child will feel more inclined to rely on parents who can admit when they were wrong.

## Helping Children to Understand Their Emotions

Children greatly appreciate it when we show them that we understand their feelings. However, we can go beyond this and actually teach them cognitive principles that will increase their own self-mastery. When children are calm and in a receptive mood, we can show them how they largely bring on their own unhappiness by their particular way of viewing events in their lives. We can explain that we all have the choice to make ourselves either happy or unhappy, depending on what we think or tell ourselves about the things which happen to us. The following example is readily understood even by a first grader:

> Life is like a big store. There are two counters in this store, one on the right and one on the left. The counter on the right has a big sign over it which says HAPPINESS. That's where we buy thoughts which make us feel good. Over the counter on the left side is a sign which says UNHAPPINESS. That's where we buy thoughts which make us feel bad. We have a choice.

107

We can decide which counter we will buy at. We can decide what we will think and how we will feel.

After giving this example, you can ask the child what kinds of thoughts are bought at the unhappiness counter, and then go on to help him identify his own upsetting thoughts. If the child has difficulty, you might suggest some likely possibilities ("Were you by any chance telling yourself . . . ?" For cognitive methods that can be easily adapted for use with children, see Chapter 1.) However, don't try to teach cognitive principles while a child is upset. A subtle way to bring these ideas home is to ask, after the child has calmed down, "What counter were you buying at before?"

# 7 Helpfulness and Consideration

In Judaism, the commandment to practice *chesed* (loving-kindness) is a major precept governing interpersonal relationships.[1] The very survival of the world is seen as dependent on *chesed*.[2] *Chesed* is not just a commendable quality but an obligation.[3] As the prophet states: "What does God require of you but to act justly, to love *chesed*, and to walk humbly with your God."[4] A person should desire to practice *chesed* whenever possible, and rejoice at the opportunity.[5]

*Chesed* has an "active" and a "passive" aspect. The former is *helpfulness* — extending ourselves to improve others' happiness or well-being; the latter, *consideration* — refraining, as the Torah enjoins us, from causing injury to someone else's feelings or property.[6] Indeed, the Talmud views this passive aspect as central to Judaism.[7] Helpfulness and consideration together constitute *chesed* — the very foundation of society. As is written in Psalms: "The world is built on *chesed*."[8]

These traits, though basic to Judaism, are not acquired automatically; parents have the responsibility to foster them in their children. This is best accomplished in two ways. First, parents must serve as an example of helpful and considerate behavior toward each other, toward their children, and toward others. This modeling, however, although essential, is not enough. Parents must also provide opportunities for their children to practice such behavior; and the home is an obvious and ideal place for such practice. By encouraging their children to help with household tasks and teaching them to avoid causing inconvenience or harm to others, parents provide early and invaluable experiences in being helpful and considerate.

In addition, children should be told of the mitzvah of *chesed* — that God wants us to feel with others and to help them whenever possible, and that helping their parents is a special form of this mitzvah, a special kind of *chesed*. This teaching, reinforced with stories of our forefathers and sages, will help to develop a strong foundation for *chesed* in the child's personality.

## Helpfulness

### BENEFITS FROM HELPFULNESS

When they request help from their children, parents must not feel that they are acting selfishly or imposing a burden. While it is true that our children's helpfulness makes things easier for us, we are at the same time giving them an opportunity to honor their parents and thereby, to fulfill this essential mitzvah. Also, we allow them to show gratitude for all that their parents do for them. Finally, love flourishes best when it expresses itself in action; and children who are taught to do things for their parents are given an opportunity to develop love for them. This point is discussed extensively in Rabbi Eliyahu Dessler's writings.[9]

Parents are obligated to help their children convert their self-centered orientation into an altruistic one — that is, to learn to love their fellow as themselves. Personality is shaped by actions;[10] the best way to develop altruism in children, therefore, is to have them do things for others. The first step in this learning process is acquired naturally in the family, when parents accustom their children to do things for them and for each other.

Practicing helpfulness at home also benefits children because it promotes a sense of self-assurance and accomplishment. As the psychologist Rudolf Dreikurs notes:

> Children should be drawn at an early age into active participation in domestic life. This promotes their social interest and the capacity for cooperation. Moreover, it strengthens their self-assurance and starts them on the way toward useful accomplishment.[11]

The members of a household are a team; each does his share, for the benefit of all. The mother's job, especially when there are small children, is often too heavy a load for one individual. In order to function effectively, a mother will need help with many of the household chores. Thus, it becomes important for parents to teach their children to participate and share in the responsibilities of the household.

## ENCOURAGING HELPFULNESS IN THE YOUNG CHILD

Young children are normally eager to assist their parents. They feel "big" and grown up when allowed to help. They are, however, naturally slow and somewhat clumsy, and sometimes their help can be more of a hindrance than a benefit. Young children are also not concerned about getting things done in the same way that adults usually are. Because they regard work as play, children are not in as much of a hurry to finish a given task. Yet parents who let themselves become impatient with young children who are trying to be helpful are apt to squelch their natural enthusiasm for helping altogether. Some parents do not permit their young children to help at all because, as one mother expressed it, "They take forever. I'd rather get it done quickly myself." Sometimes a child who wants to help is told, "No, you can't do it. You'll make a mess." Such treatment is a pity, for the child is thus denied the many benefits helpfulness brings. It may also make it more difficult to accustom the child to helping when he is older and more capable. Parents with this attitude should learn to tolerate some inconvenience and disruption of their routine, so that in the long run everyone will benefit.

Even a very young child can be allowed to help, for instance, with bringing dishes to the sink or wiping off the table. By the time they are five or six, most children are quite capable of washing dishes and will be eager to do this as well. A stepstool will be needed, or the child can kneel on a chair. It is worth it for parents to spend time on this kind of training, which is relatively easy to accomplish while the child is still young. Later, these habits are much more difficult to establish.

One young mother was asked why her children so greatly enjoyed helping with the cooking. She answered, "My children always saw my work in the kitchen as play. At a very young age I allowed them to be with me in the kitchen to join in 'Mommy's playing.' I gave them all kinds of things to do — whatever they could — even slicing tomatoes.   To this day they love cooking."

As mentioned before, children naturally love to help with chores; however, they can come to regard it as a burden — often under the negative influence of the adults around them. In the Torah view, work is of central importance;[12] it is seen as our completion of God's creation.[13] Shema'yah, mentor of the renowned sage Hillel, teaches that one should love work.[14] This obligates us to nurture such love in our children by letting our own happy and cheerful attitude toward work be an example to them. Parents sometimes refrain from asking for much help from their children, telling themselves, "Let them enjoy life while they are young; they'll have enough responsibilities when they get older." This attitude is not conducive to developing the love for working and doing which is the Torah ideal.

## MANNER OF REQUESTING HELP

The way we request the child's help critically affects his even-
tual attitude toward helping. It is better to avoid prefacing our
request with "I want you to . . ." as this places our wishes too
much at the center. A friendly, matter-of-fact manner of
requesting is best: "Please take this garbage down" rather than
"Be a darling and take this garbage down for me please."
Requests such as "Would you mind cracking these eggs for
me" or "If it isn't too much trouble, could you diaper the baby"
should be strongly avoided; these convey a sense of unsureness, both about the child's willingness to help and about the
parent's right to ask to begin with. Similarly, "Come and help
me with the dishes" is better than "Do you want to help me
with the dishes?"; if the child answers "No," you're in trouble.
In fact, it isn't always necessary to ask directly for help. One
can say, for instance, "Saree, you can set the table for supper"
or "Come Yonah — you can help me slice the cucumbers." At
times we can suggest, "It would be helpful if you would . . ."

Never plead with a child. Also, don't tell him how tired you
are; this sounds apologetic. Simply say, "I need your help."
Parents should not feel that they have to give a reason for
requesting help.

This take-it-for-granted attitude toward helping was neatly summed up by one mother of eight:

> When the children were little, there was just no
> question about their helping — I couldn't manage
> otherwise. It was understood. Each child had his job
> and it was taken for granted that everyone had to do
> his share. The kids seem to have absorbed this
> attitude — that I expected it of them — after all, I
> couldn't do everything!

Even when parents are tired or rushed, they must make
the effort to ask for the child's assistance calmly and pleasantly. Parents should be careful, when asking for help, that

113

their tone of voice does not convey any resentment, annoyance, or anxiety. A sharp "Come in here and clear this table," for example, could reveal resentment toward the child because he does not help enough. The hidden criticism in the parent's request is picked up by the child, who might feel offended and be unwilling to help. On the other hand, a hesitant manner of requesting, as mentioned above, reveals the parent's anxiety that the child might not want to help; often enough, the outcome is the very thing the parent fears. It is worthwhile for parents to learn to control these harmful emotions by identifying and changing the attitudes which trigger them.

## SHOWING APPRECIATION

Parents should express appreciation when their children have been helpful. They thereby demonstrate the proper and desirable response when one person has helped another, effectively modeling *hakarath tovah* (gratefulness). Effusive displays of gratitude, however, are inappropriate and may make the child suspicious that his help was not really expected, as opposed to the take-it-for-granted attitude mentioned above. He may also come to depend on such praise and believe that any contribution he makes deserves high commendation. He could even develop a need for constant approval of all his actions, not only from his parents but from others in his environment as well. A simple "thanks" should suffice for a small task, and even this is not always necessary for chores performed routinely.

Care should be taken that in expressing appreciation, the child's helpfulness is not linked to his character. Like exaggerated praise, expressions such as "You are a good girl for helping me" may well lead to a child's helping in order to be liked and gain approval. In contrast, with objective praise such as "You worked hard and did a nice job" or "You were very helpful today" or "You did it gladly — you felt happy to do the mitzvah," the child will come to perceive the intrinsic value of his behavior.

Keep praise realistic. Children feel uncomfortable with praise which is neither true nor deserved. It may even, in fact, trigger misbehavior — the child realizes he is not the "wonderful boy" you claimed he is, and hastens to prove that he cannot live up to this image.

## ASSIGNMENT OF CHORES

While some parents manage well by asking for help when it is needed, others find that it works better to assign routine jobs regularly in advance. In this way, each child knows what is expected of him, and the need to ask for help is greatly reduced. For example, the serving of courses at the Shabbath table can be assigned to various children beforehand. Charts listing each child's chores for the week are very useful; they prevent much unnecessary arguing over whose turn it is to do a chore next. The children should be allowed to participate in setting up such charts, as in other decisions concerning delegation of tasks. They are more likely to accept their obligations cheerfully when they are given a choice in the matter. The mother can begin by gathering all the children together and telling them, for instance, "There are many different jobs that have to be done in the house. It's a little too much for Mommy to do by herself, and she needs your help. Let's make a list of what you children can do."

Mothers can usually rely on their common sense to help them decide what can be expected of children at various ages. However, if they are unsure, they can discuss it with another, more experienced mother. Those who are skeptical about the capacities of very young children may want to read about the amazing accomplishments in Montessori schools, where children of three learn to sweep, serve hot soup, and polish silver — all part of their training in the "exercises of practical life."

Since children generally dislike doing the same job every

day, most families adopt a rotation system, with different jobs for each child for every day of the week (see samples). Separate charts can be made for Erev and Motzaei Shabbath (Shabbath eve and the night following Shabbath). Pictures can be drawn for younger children who have not yet learned to read. In some families it works out well for an older child to be given the job of supervisor; this relieves the mother from having to check to see if chores were properly done. Older children can take over making of charts as well, dividing chores as they see fit. A self-monitoring system is a good idea; the child puts a checkmark next to his name after he has completed all his chores. If the chart is made up with a marker and the checks put in with a pencil, there is no problem with erasing them at the end of each week.

### DAILY ROTATION CHART

| JOB | SUN. | MON. | TUES. | WED. | THURS. |
|---|---|---|---|---|---|
| peel vegetables set table | Tamar | Elly | Rachel | Naomi | Chaim |
| clear & clean table sweep floor | Chaim | Tamar | Elly | Rachel | Naomi |
| wash dishes * | Naomi | Chaim | Tamar | Elly | Rachel |
| dry dishes empty garbage | Rachel | Naomi | Chaim | Tamar | Elly |
| prepare lunch boxes | Elly | Rachel | Naomi | Chaim | Tamar |

*If there is a dishwasher, loading and emptying it could be one job.

Some mothers prefer to have certain jobs done by the same child every day. In this case, individual lists can be made up for each child. Another method is to attach the children's names to a bulletin board and post underneath them each day a slip of paper with jobs for that day. A board with a wipe-off surface can be used as well.

### WEEKLY ROTATION CHART

| JOB | WEEK 1 | WEEK 2 | WEEK 3 | WEEK 4 |
|---|---|---|---|---|
| basement toys helping with baby | Ruthy | Shuly | Debby | Yitzy |
| kitchen helping | Shuly | Debby | Yitzy | Ruthy |
| laundry | Debby | Yitzy | Ruthy | Shuly |
| errands | Yitzy | Ruthy | Shuly | Debby |

While charts are a big help, we will still need to request help with less routine jobs. One mother with a large family relates:

> I need only to call out, "There are vegetables to peel. Anyone have time?" There is always someone ready to do it. Similarly, when we need bread I announce, "We're out of bread. Who can go to the store?" Every morning I prepare a list of items to be bought at the grocer's; the first one ready does the shopping.

This mother finds that this system works well for her; for others, it works out better to turn to one child and assign him the task.

**WORKWHEEL FOR KITCHEN CHORES**

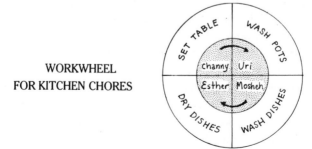

Workwheel reprinted by permission of Grosset & Dunlap from LIBERATED PARENTS/LIBERATED CHILDREN by Adele Faber and Elaine Mazlish, © 1974 by Adele Faber and Elaine Mazlish.

Sometimes children who think they are given more than their share of tasks complain, "It's not fair! Why do you always ask me?" Parents, rather than responding defensively to such accusations, should proceed as if the child's perception is valid. A wise parent will not try to prove the child wrong, but might simply reply, "You seem to feel that I ask you more often than the others. We'll talk about it later, but for now, please do what I asked anyway." Later, at an opportune time, the parent could initiate a discussion — remembering not to argue with the child or to respond defensively. Some empathy, with assurances that you try to be fair, will reassure him. The parent might also use this opportunity to discuss with the child any disrespect which he may have shown earlier. If, however, the child's complaint is justified, the parent should resolve to distribute chores more carefully in the future. This does not, however, warrant undue concern. Overzealous attempts to be fair invariably help bring about the very jealousy they are intended to prevent.

There is an understandable tendency for parents to request help more often from children with a positive attitude than from those who show reluctance. However, in addition to reinforcing the attitude of the reluctant child, this can lead to resentment and a negative attitude in the child who wants to help but now sees the situation as unfair. Here, it is worth making the effort not to take the easy way out. In general, unpleasant as it may be, parents should see to it that the reluctant child does his fair share of work.

In every family there is bound to be some unevenness in distribution of chores. Obviously, younger children are given less to do than older ones. A high-school age child preparing for regents examinations or a child approaching bar mitzvah might temporarily be allowed to devote all his spare time to studying. Since boys have a special obligation to study Torah, we will want to encourage them in this; if we need help and the boy is occupied in Torah study, we will, whenever possible, ask a daughter to help instead. If parents notice resentment in a child who is required to do more because of such extenuating circumstances, they should explain the situation and do their best to help the child accept it.

## RELUCTANCE TO HELP

Reluctance to help is quite normal in children. Many parents, however, are troubled by such a show of displeasure. They want their child to be happy, and dislike forcing him to help when he clearly doesn't want to. Often, unpleasant memories of being forced to help when they were children are at the bottom of such parents' reluctance. Or, they may fear the child's coming to resent them. Thus, when a request for help is met with reluctant compliance, these parents are apt to say something like, "You don't have to do it if you don't really want to" — which, unfortunately, does nothing to encourage further cooperation. Still other parents so dread the fuss that might ensue that they refrain from asking for help for that reason alone, preferring to do things themselves much to the detriment of all concerned.

More commonly, parents react to the child's reluctance to help with annoyance. They may scold, for example, "Why do you make a face — don't you want to help?" and "Aren't you ashamed that you want to leave me with all the dishes!" — or, with obvious bitterness, "Never mind — I'll do it myself." This, however, only makes the child feel resentful and even less inclined to help. Such complaining and criticizing most often results in the child's internalizing our negative view of him, and in establishing as a fact that he does not want to help. It is as if the parents have pinned on the child a label which says: "I don't want to help. I am bad."

Many parents, fully aware that their scolding and criticizing do no good, berate themselves relentlessly for their non-constructive conduct. Instead, they should remind themselves that people, including children and especially older ones, do not readily change long established behavior patterns. Even if parents cease to criticize their child and adopt more effective methods of requesting his help, it does not guarantee that the child will promptly change his attitude. If he does not, it can be very difficult for parents to avoid falling back into their old habits of disapproving and complaining. They may then begin to evaluate the child poorly, or to see themselves as having failed as parents.

Therefore, rather than paying any attention to displays of displeasure at having to help, it is best for parents to learn to ignore these completely. When a child, for example, offers obvious excuses such as "I'm too tired" or "I have too much homework" (watch your own similar statements — the child may just be copying them!) we can show understanding but still, in a friendly way, insist that the job be done. We might respond, for instance, "I know you're tired, but peel the potatoes anyway." A loving stroke on the cheek as we say this can work wonders. Even when a child actually refuses to do a job, saying "I don't want to" or "I don't feel like it," our response should still be as before. Answers such as "What do you mean you don't want to do it? I said so and that's that!" should be strictly avoided. Later we must explain to the child, very quietly, that he is not allowed to refuse his parents' requests. Another way of handling such refusals is to say to the child, "Shall I do it?" However, this must be said very softly or it can have the wrong effect. Naturally, a parent has to judge whether this approach will work with his particular child.

While we would certainly prefer it if the child did his tasks gladly, we must learn to be satisfied for the time being so long as he actually does them. However, don't say to a grumbling child, "I don't expect you to love washing the dishes, all I expect is that you do it" or "I don't care if you don't like emptying the garbage, you have to do it anyway." This only reinforces his negative attitude. If we consistently ignore all signs of displeasure and maintain a pleasant but firm manner, the child's attitude is likely to eventually improve. Even though he may never learn to exactly enjoy doing dishes, he will come to see it as an opportunity to fulfill the mitzvah of honoring his parents. He will also feel the satisfaction which comes from participating and doing his share, and the knowledge that he is able to do something for his parents in return for all they do for him.

A serious talk with the child can be very helpful too. We might say to him: "You know, doing what Mommy and Daddy ask is a big mitzvah. Part of the mitzvah is the happiness you give us when we see that you're glad to do it. But when you show us you don't feel like helping, it makes us unhappy. Then even though you do it in the end, your mitzvah is much smaller." One mother related how touched she was by her eight-year-old daughter's response to being told, "I feel bad when you tell me that you don't want to do what I've asked." At first she replied only, rather thoughtfully, "I didn't know that." Later she came and asked, "Why didn't you tell me before that you feel bad?"

Parents must never say to a child who shows reluctance to help: "Okay, don't come asking me to do anything for you," or, when he asks for some favor: "You don't want to do things for me, so I don't want to do anything for you either." This is not only vengeful, but non-constructive as well. Parents should also avoid any mulling over the child's supposed ingratitude: "After all I do for him he doesn't even want to do a little bit for me in return!" This will only build up resentment toward him. Parents should instead try to view his reluctance to help as a sign of poor inner discipline.

Nevertheless, there are situations where it works out well when the reluctant child is left alone. One mother whose older daughter was unusually helpful, whereas her younger daughter was much less cooperative, decided against insisting that the second daughter do her share. She reasoned, "When the older girl leaves the house and she sees that I need her help, she'll pitch in gladly." Several years later when her older sister got married, the younger daughter indeed changed dramatically for the better, gladly helping out with all the household

121

chores and with caring for the younger children. This is a case of the power of optimistic expectations: the daughter realized that the mother expected that she would not let her down when her help was really needed.

Sometimes parents pay or reward their children to motivate them to do their chores. As mentioned in Chapter 4, rewards can be useful for instilling basic good behavior; but they have serious drawbacks when used to bring about compliance with chores, which children should learn to see as an expected contribution to the household. Rewards for chores, quite to the contrary, can develop in children an attitude of "What do I get for this" — to the point, sometimes, that they may refuse to do tasks without a reward. Moreover, rewarding or paying children for doing chores sets the parent-child relationship in distorted perspective. Children receive everything they need from their parents; let them do what they can to show their appreciation. As Rabbi Yoel Schwartz writes:

> [The child] must know that going to the grocery store or taking out the garbage are his obligation both because he must honor his parents and because he should contribute his part to the family enterprise. If we promise him candy or money, we block his developing this sense of obligation.[15]

Novel ways can often be found to motivate children to do the jobs they dislike. As one mother related:

> My children always liked hanging and taking down laundry, but no one wanted to fold it. So I said to them one day, "Come, let's play 'Personalities' while we fold the laundry." Everyone had a good time and gradually they learned to enjoy doing it.

## NEGLIGENCE IN TAKING CARE OF CHORES

Some children, while they may not initially show reluctance to help, instead avoid doing their chores by procrastinating or "forgetting." Discovering that a chore has been left undone can be annoying to parents. Again, however, outbursts at the child such as "Why do I have to be constantly after you to do everything!" are counterproductive. Instead, parents in this predicament must learn to view their child's procrastinating behavior not as a sign of bad character, but as a bad habit. They can proceed to teach the child to change his behavior.

For instance, they can explain to him, maintaining a very low voice, "You know, when Daddy or I ask you to do something, you should take care of it right away and not make us remind you. Doing what we ask is your mitzvah. Now, if you're in the middle of something, you can always ask, 'Can I finish this first?' and I'll usually say okay. But otherwise, jobs have to be done right away."

Procrastination, of course, is a tenacious habit, and the child will not get over it right away. Parents must be patient; they should refrain from telling the child "Please don't make me remind you so often to do what I asked" as this is frequently received as a complaint. Even the word please, when given a certain emphasis, can convey plenty of annoyance: "Will yo·· *please* go in and do those dishes." Parents must also avoid letting the child's negligence make them feel powerless; the child usually senses this and it strongly affects the way he responds to them.

Instead, parents must keep their cool and give quiet, consistent reminders. With the occasionally negligent child, cuing is often a helpful technique. For instance, a child who was supposed to sweep a room can be quietly handed the broom. Sometimes a word or two will suffice — "Aaron, the dishes." Notes, too, can serve as reminders; they can be "delivered" via a brother or sister. Charts also offer good opportunities for cuing; when a child has forgotten to empty the garbage we can tell him, "Take a look at the chart and see what job you were supposed to do."

As for the consistently negligent child, who ends up doing very little work often much to the resentment of his siblings, he must be reminded in a friendly way that the family is a team with everyone doing his share. The importance of cooperation and of everyone pitching in must be stressed to him gently but firmly.

While we should in general exercise patience, we might on occasion decide to do the work ourselves when it is too inconvenient to wait. The child should not be made to feel guilty about this. If he comes to tell us "I was going to do it" we can answer, "I'm sorry but I couldn't wait."

Sometimes a procrastinating child will "progress" from not doing chores at all to doing them poorly. If so, parents should not hesitate to check up on his work and ask him to repeat a poorly done chore. It is best to stick to objective evaluations and descriptions, telling the child directly and simply what you want him to do — "This floor was not swept well. Please do it over." It is a good practice to first, whenever possible, find something good to say about the work — "Hmm — let me see this pot. Nice job. But this cover is still dirty. Please go over it once more." Parents should not, of course, expect perfection; if they do say anything critical, it should be constructive — "I think you can do a better job than this."

At the same time, parents should avoid hovering over the child to make sure he is doing everything properly. Children need to sense that we have confidence in them and expect them to do a good job. For instance, when children help with cooking, they may not always notice bits of food or peels which drop to the floor while they work. It is disagreeable for us and the child if we badger him to pick these up. Here a simple "There are some egg shells on the floor" or "A few apple peels dropped over there" will do very well.

## FLEXIBILITY

Although it is generally best to accustom children to doing what we ask of them right away, there is room for flexibility. We can teach a child to ask, when he wants to postpone a particular job, "Can this wait a few minutes?" or "Can I first do (such and such)?" But when our answer is no, we should stick to it and permit no arguments.

A child may sometimes have a legitimate reason for finding it difficult to help. Nevertheless, since it is wrong for him to refuse to do what his parents request, he should be taught, in such situations, to express himself appropriately. For instance, if he is truly overburdened with school work, a proper way to express this would be, "I'm just loaded down with homework. Is it okay if I don't go to the store?" Parents can safely assume that the child's reason is legitimate, especially if he is normally happy to help and does so without complaint.

A readiness to compromise once in a while is important. Thus we might offer to do some of the dishes if the job seems like too much for the child. If a particular task doesn't have to be taken care of right away, we can let the child decide when to do it. Empathy is important too. One mother told the following story:

> I asked my son to set the table and fill the pepper cases with cheese. He cried, "It's too hard — I can't do it!" Formerly I would have responded, "It's easy — I'm sure you can do it" or "This is what I asked you to do and you have to do it." An argument would then ensue and often I would end up doing it myself rather than make a fuss. This time I remembered to be empathic. I said to him, "You think it's too hard for you to do that. I'll tell you what — go ahead and start and see how you do. If you have trouble I'll help you." He calmed down immediately and began to fill the cases.

Parents frequently give in to a child's protestations about a job being too hard because of their uncertainty whether it is indeed too much for him. Usually, however, there is no basis for such doubt; rather, the parents' uncertainty is rooted in self-critical attitudes. Parents can avoid such quandaries by making certain in their own minds, before making their request, that the child is capable of doing the task. In any case, as mentioned in Chapter 3, parents should not worry excessively about this but simply try to do their best.

*Regard for the child's needs.* Another important aspect of flexibility is to show consideration toward the child and his needs. If, for instance, parents find it necessary to interrupt a child who is engrossed in some activity, they should express their regret at having to do so. To a child who is preparing for a test one might say, "I'm sorry to have to interrupt you while you're studying, but I need your help." It is a good idea to give a child advance warning — "When you're finished with this game, I'll need your help with folding the diapers."

How far should the parents' consideration toward their child go? Should parents, for example, release an ambitious child from his obligations to help at home and permit him to devote his time to his studies exclusively? Should they forego an older daughter's help and allow her to spend many hours with her friends, preparing an elaborate and impressive graduation exhibit at school? In answering these questions, we should weigh the relative importance of the alternatives involved. What is more important — the five or so extra points on the examination, or taking some of the workload off an overburdened mother? While extracurricular activities may be a source of much genuine pleasure to the child, they should not take precedence over parents who need help. Even when the activities serve a charitable purpose, it should not be forgotten that "charity begins at home." In the words of the prophet, "Do not hide yourself from your own flesh."[16]

# Consideration

In his summation of the entire Torah as "That which is hateful to you, do not do to your fellow," the sage Hillel aptly expressed the fundamental role consideration plays in Judaism.[17] Consideration means regard for others' emotional well-being as well as belongings; it is an attitude that should govern our entire manner of relating to people. When our sages portray the ideal person who by his example attracts others to Torah, they mention only two traits, which suggest a person marked by consideration for others: "His dealings are faithful and his conversation with people is gentle."[18]

Lessons in consideration, as in so many other character traits, begin at home. For parents, this means both teaching the children how to behave considerately, and modeling consideration in their own behavior toward each other as well as the children. If, for instance, a child is studying with the light on in the room when her sister wants to sleep, the parents should not complain unthinkingly, "Why do you keep the light on — can't you see your sister wants to sleep!" but should say softly, "Your sister needs to sleep. How about studying in another room." Inconsiderate behavior outside the home should be handled with equal calm. A child who pushes ahead in a bus line, for example, can be quietly told, "Let's let these people get on first — they were here before us."

## TEACHING CONSIDERATION

*Returning objects.* Children frequently neglect to return objects to their proper place. While this may greatly inconvenience the parents, they will more effectively handle the situation if they manage to control their annoyance. For example, a father discovers that his pliers are missing from the tool chest. Rather than angrily calling out "Who took my pliers? Can't you people put things back where they belong!" he could quietly ask each child, "Have you seen my pliers?" When the child who borrowed the pliers produces them, the father might say to him, "I guess you forgot to put them back. Next time, please try to remember." At some opportune time, the father could discuss with the child the importance of returning whatever is borrowed, explaining that failure to do so inconveniences others, wasting their time with needless searching. He can also, if appropriate, remind the child that he must ask permission before borrowing anything. By thus refraining from showing any personal annoyance, the father can successfully focus the child's attention on an important educational lesson: the harm we cause others through our neglect.

When children persist in failing to return borrowed objects to their place, they can be refused permission to use them. For example, if the child has neglected for the third time to return his father's screwdriver to the tool cabinet, he can be told: "I'm really sorry but I can't let you borrow my screwdriver for the time being. This is the third time you forgot to return it." If he then takes it anyway, some appropriate punishment is in order.

One mother, whose kitchen shears were forever disappearing from the drawer despite the fact that each child had his own scissors, tried tying a note to the shears: "Please return these to the drawer after using." When this did not help, she changed the note to: "These are not to be taken out of the kitchen." After that the shears remained in their place.

*Cleaning up messes.* Another way children can cause parents considerable inconvenience is by leaving messes for someone else (usually the mother) to clean up. Rather than thinking with irritation, "They shouldn't leave me their messes like this!" parents should concentrate on how to remedy the situation. A child who, for example, leaves spilled milk on the counter can be calmly handed the rag and asked to clean it up. If he wants to first finish the sandwich he fixed himself, he should be told, very pleasantly, "Please do it now. I can't work on the counter this way."

Older children who come in at odd hours and do not always eat with the family should be expected to clean up after themselves. However, they are likely to forget at times; if so, it is best to call the child in and tell him quietly, "You forgot to clean up." On the other hand, parents should avoid being excessively fussy. They should not make it a practice to clean up after their children, but they should be able to overlook a bit here and there.

For a detailed discussion of order and cleanliness, see the next chapter.

*Understanding parents' needs.* Children can be taught that parents' needs go beyond wanting a neat and orderly house. When a mother requires some quiet, or a chance to get her work done without the children underfoot, there is nothing wrong with explaining this quietly and pleasantly to her children. For example: "Kids, I need some time to take care of this pile of laundry and prepare supper — please play in your room now"; "I have to get this work done now — later when I'm finished I'll come to you."

A mother may have a headache, or be exhausted after a long night up with the baby. If she waits to talk to the children until her nerves are totally frayed, she will then find it difficult to remain calm. A simple explanation such as, "Children, I have a bad headache, you'll have to leave me alone for a while now" will suffice.

It is particularly important that we deal calmly with children when we are under pressure, such as on Erev Shabbath or before Pesach. If the children continually come into the kitchen for drinks or snacks while things are hectic, have a "no snacking" rule for such times and maintain it pleasantly but firmly. Or, so that children won't need to come into the kitchen, they can be given a bowl of apples and something to drink in their room. Naturally, older children should be in the kitchen to help, with the exception of the one who occupies the little ones or takes them out for a walk. If a mother finishes with the cooking well before candle-lighting time on Erev Shabbath and wants the children to remember to stay out so the kitchen will remain clean, she can post a sign on the door: "KITCHEN CLOSED UNTIL SHABBATH."

Often, parents have difficulty with children who disturb them at night, either to come into their bed or sometimes to request a drink or something to eat. The important thing is to be firm from the very beginning and not permit children to come into our room and certainly not into the bed. We must explain to them that a child is not permitted to wake a parent unless, of course, for something really important. It is worthwhile to discuss with children what is important and what is not. During this training period it may sometimes be necessary to lead the child back to his room and tuck him firmly into his bed.

When children have developed a habit of disturbing their parents at night, there are things that can be done. A lock on the door can prevent children from coming in. If children persist in knocking on the door and creating a general disturbance, we might try using incentives to rid them of this habit. Tell them in the evening at bedtime that they will get a surprise in the morning if they refrain from bothering us at night. The surprise should be something small, such as a few nuts or a special breakfast cereal.

The problem of drinks at night can be solved by leaving a covered cup of water in the room. Food should not be given at night.

*Visits and phone conversations.* To what extent can a mother expect her child to let her chat with others without continual interruptions? Many mothers are in conflict over this, fearing that they may be harming their child by ignoring his demands for attention at such times. Children, in turn, have an uncanny way of sensing this conflict, and can make the mother miserable with ceaseless attempts to get her attention.

It is not necessary, however, to be in conflict. Children do not need constant attention, and will manage very well without it for a surprisingly long time — provided we expect it of them. Keep in mind that if we stop talking in order to give the child attention every time he interrupts, we reinforce his behavior. Stopping repeatedly to tell the child "You're interrupting" has a similar effect.

Children can be taught to permit us to converse with other adults. When meeting an acquaintance while out with the child, we can tell him, very pleasantly, "Let me talk to my friend for a few minutes." When a guest arrives, we can explain that we will be busy for a while with the visitor. If the child comes to tell us something we can say, "Excuse me, I'm talking right now to (so and so)" or "Is this very important or can it wait?"

We can, of course, show the child small tokens of attention to assure him that we have not forgotten him. If he comes over to tell us something we can stroke his cheek, stop a moment to smile or nod — just enough to satisfy him. We can also take notice of him in small ways here and there.

If a child's disruptive behavior when there are visitors has persisted for a long time, you will have to go through an initial training period. The child will keep trying hard to get your attention as you converse; but you must continue to give him only token signs of attention. If he cries and seems very unhappy, you might take him in your arms to soothe him, but still go on calmly with the conversation. Comments such as "He never leaves me any peace" should be strictly avoided; as should asking the child, "Can't you leave us alone for a while?"

The phone can also pose a problem. Unlike when the parent is talking to a visitor, the child does not see the person on the other side of the line and is therefore less aware of it when he interrupts. It is best to stop the conversation for a moment and tell the child, "Please wait a few minutes — I'm on the phone" or simply, "I'm on the phone now." Don't protest loudly at him. Children can be told that they should interrupt phone conversations only for something important. However, it is unrealistic to expect the child to wait too long. There is nothing wrong with saying "I have to close our conversation now — my children need me." Some mothers disconnect their telephone every day for an hour or so to devote some exclusive time to their children.

## MANNERS

Manners and politeness are an aspect of consideration which the Talmudic sages considered so important that they devoted two minor tractates (*Derekh Eretz Rabbah* and *Zuta*) to the subject. There are those who disdain manners as automatic or superficial rituals; and while they can be taken too far, without manners our lives would lack the extra friendliness and warmth that are so important in human relationships.

We teach the young child pleasant manners primarily by our good example; and also by occasional friendly prompting. For example, if the child says "I'm hungry — I want a cracker," we can quietly ask him to say instead, "May I have a cracker please"; or we can prompt, "How can you say that nicely?" Children should be taught that thanking others is not only good manners but is meritorious as it shows *hakarath tovah*. We should also explain to the child that we are obliged to both greet and respond to the greetings of people we know when we encounter them.[19] Teaching children to speak pleasantly to others is another aspect of good manners which should not be overlooked.

A child's lack of manners can be a sensitive spot for parents. Many parents are highly conscious of what others think of them. When a child publicly displays poor manners, they fear that he will make a bad impression and thereby reflect poorly on themselves. If, for instance, the child does not take a proffered hand, they will rush to make excuses. As effective educators, however, we must learn not to concern ourselves with others' unjustified poor opinion of us. The learning of manners takes time, and the child's lack does not necessarily imply any failure on the parents' part.

The parents' concern over their child's lack of manners may express itself in continual prompting of the child to be polite. Although this may be momentarily effective, a child who is regularly reminded to "Say please" or "Tell the lady thank you for the raisins" is unlikely to internalize politeness. Indeed, with a child who requests impolitely, relying on "Ask nicely and I'll give it to you" simply teaches him to respond to your cues, so that he remembers his manners only after being prompted.

A more constructive approach is to explain to the child, when you are alone with him, why courtesy is desirable. You might say, for instance, "There are lots of ways to ask for things. How does it sound when I say 'Pass the butter' or 'Bring me a glass of water.' It sounds like I'm giving you orders, doesn't it? But how about if I say it this way: 'Please pass the butter' or 'Would you please bring me a glass of water.' That sounds much nicer, doesn't it?" This kind of modeling is particularly effective.

Many parents are especially embarrassed by a child's asking for food in someone else's house. Again, they should not respond on the spot, but should let the child get the requested food (or drink); only afterwards, on the way home or at home, should the matter be discussed. It should be explained to the child that he must wait for food until offered; if he is thirsty, however, he may ask for water.

Role playing is another useful teaching method. For example, in anticipation of a visit from Grandmother, who is certain to bring a gift for her grandchild, a mother might rehearse with the child as follows:

Mother: Grandma will be here soon for a visit — she'll probably bring you a present. Let's practice how you'll thank her. You be Grandma — go out and ring the bell — I'll make believe I'm you. (Child goes out and rings bell; mother opens the door, prompts the child to say "Hello")
Child: Hello.
Mother: (acting as child) Hi Grandma. (again prompts child)

> Child: I brought you a present.
> Mother: Thank you, Grandma.

The roles are then reversed, with the mother acting as the grandmother and the child as himself. When the role play is over, the mother can say to the child, "That was very nice. Grandma will be pleased when you thank her so politely." The commendation, if the child behaved as was practiced, should be repeated after the visit; for example, "It was nice the way you thanked Grandma for the present before."

*Interrupting.* Our sages take a dim view of those who interrupt others, even referring to one who does so as a "clod."[20] Children interrupt impulsively, and must be taught to allow others to finish speaking before they themselves speak. As well as being worthwhile in itself, this provides good practice in learning self-control. Parents must be patient and must not rebuke a child with "You're not letting me finish"; better to say pleasantly, "Please let me finish." They should be prepared to keep asserting themselves gently but firmly until the child learns not to interrupt.

Likewise, when several children are standing around us, each interrupting the other and all wanting to be heard at the same time, we can say, good-naturedly, "Kids, I'd like to hear what all of you have to tell me but I can listen to only one person at a time. Suppose we take turns. We'll start with . . ."

*Table manners.* Teaching table manners requires persistence with most young children. They need to be taught that it is forbidden to behave in a way that disgusts others.[21] They should be shown how to use a spoon and fork as soon as possible, and encouraged to do so. Still, parents should not be too fussy or demanding; they should strictly avoid comments like "Look how you're eating!" or "You're eating like a pig!" A word here and there is enough; and when a child tries hard to eat well he should be complimented, which will encourage him and may also motivate the other children to emulate him.

A nice way to remind a child who uses his fingers instead of his knife is to simply point to the knife or quietly hand it to him. It helps sometimes to set aside a few minutes at mealtime for paying special attention to manners.

## THOUGHTFULNESS

We can require and teach children to be considerate of others' needs for order, cleanliness, and quiet. More difficult to instill is thoughtfulness, the positive counterpart of consideration. It is the ability to sense what will give others pleasure and satisfaction and act on it. Thoughtfulness is so difficult to teach because it must be self-motivated. Modeling is necessary, but parents can also encourage thoughtful deeds which the child initiates. When an older child, for instance, offers to watch the baby so his mother can rest, she can accept with a pleased "That's very thoughtful of you." Parents can also sometimes suggest small acts of thoughtfulness. A mother could, for example, hint to her son, "Your brother is late for school this morning. How about making his bed for him?" A subsequent commendation of the child's thoughtfulness reinforces his behavior.

Giving appropriate compliments is a form of thoughtfulness too. Parents can try to make their child aware of situations where compliments are appreciated. Modeling is particularly effective here. A father can, for example, make a point of praising his wife's cooking while the family is seated at the Shabbath table. Then, while the mother is in the kitchen, he can tell the children, "Isn't the soup delicious? Let's tell Mommy; that will make her feel good."

While a mild reproof for a child's failure to show thoughtfulness may at times be beneficial, outbursts such as "Why can't you do something, for once, *without* being asked!" will only arouse the child's ill will. Most children, if properly trained to be helpful and considerate, will eventualy begin to behave thoughtfully as well.

# 8 Orderliness and Cleanliness

Disorder causes much waste of time, as well as inconvenience. Habits of orderliness not only enable us to function productively, they help us develop an organized and efficient mind — "for the person is shaped by his actions."[1] In the list of outstanding characteristics of our greatest sages, Rabbi Akiva is praised for his beautifully ordered mind.[2] (Perhaps it was this trait that qualified him to lay the foundation for the entire Talmud.)[3] The story is told of a rabbi who traveled many miles to his son's yeshivah to see how the boy's learning was progressing. When he arrived he came first to his son's room. After noting merely that the room was organized and tidy, the father left, certain that the boy was learning well.[4]

Parents should foster an attitude of "It's our house; we work together to keep it ordered and clean." Some mothers regard their children as more or less a hindrance to their efforts. This attitude leads to reproaches such as "Look what you're doing to my clean kitchen floor!" This is not the way to develop a spirit of cooperation and teamwork.

## Early Training

One of the first ways to teach a child order is to show him how to put his toys away. The mother can suggest to him that each toy has its place: "Let's put the train set here; the puzzles can go over here. . . ." A low shelf is advisable; it is more conducive to organization than a toy chest into which all toys are tossed. Toys with many parts should be kept in sturdy boxes or plastic containers such as are used in kindergartens. Large Clorox bottles with their tops cut off also make good containers. Since small children will frequently wish to play near their mother, it is helpful to have a cart with select toys that can be wheeled in and out of the child's room. Or, a plastic clothes basket can be used; the child himself pulls it from room to room for playing and quick pickups.

Young children will enjoy putting their toys away if we teach them to regard it as a sort of game. Children generally get much satisfaction from creating order in their environment. However, we must give them time and not demand perfection. If there is no older brother or sister to help the child, the mother should work together with him at first, gradually doing less and less until he can do the whole job by himself. Comments such as "How nice the room looks now!" heighten the child's feeling of pleasure and help to develop a love of order. Our cheerful manner as we help him instills a positive attitude, too. By the time they are four, most children no longer need help with cleaning up; however, we should still be willing to lend a hand at times.

Since it is unreasonable to expect that a child's room always be in order, parents should establish a regular time at which rooms must be tidied. Before supper is usually best. This way we do not have to constantly remind a child to straighten his room, which can bring him to view neatness as a burden. However, to give them enough time children should be reminded well in advance. A timer set for about fifteen minutes gives them an idea how long they have left and discourages dawdling. When they are finished, mother is called to inspect. Comments such as "Nice job" or "I'll tell Daddy this evening what a good job you did" are encouraging to the child. If the room's appearance is not as it should be, we can point out what still needs to be done. Supper is served only when everything is in order.

Even though a special time is set aside for cleanup, a child should still be taught to preserve some semblance of order in his room while playing. For instance, there can be a rule that no more than two toys be taken out to play with at one time. Toys with many small parts can be kept in boxes on an upper shelf so that the children cannot get at them without asking specially.

All of this may not be so simple when there are several children, some of whom are inclined to be neat and others less so. A tidy child is apt to become annoyed with his less orderly brother or sister. Should he complain about the state of his room, the mother can take him aside and understandingly tell him, for example, "I know it bothers you when your sister leaves her toys all over the room, but it doesn't help to get annoyed. Why don't you just remind her quietly to put a few things away."

The wise parent does not become involved in discussions about who took out which toy. Rather, tidying the room should be considered a joint effort. However, when an older and a younger child share the room, the older one can be made responsible for cleaning it up. It is well to encourage a spirit of friendly cooperation among the children. If one child protests, for example, "I didn't take the blocks out — why should I put them away!" the parent can respond, with a smile, "I know, but put them back anyway." When the child has friends over to play, he can be reminded to ask the other children to help with cleanup before they go home.

Children should also be taught to keep their clothing in order. Even a young child can learn to bring dirty clothes to the hamper; older children can fold or hang up worn clothing as well. Here again the mother should assist the child when first teaching him, and can encourage him with comments such as, "It's good when the room is in order; then we can find everything easily."

A child should also be required, as soon as he is capable, to make his bed. When children are still too young, older children can be asked to do it for them. Even if it means a child will be late for school a few times, rules about making beds should be upheld. (Of course, the situation is more complicated if the child goes to school by bus or other transportation; see "When the Child Relies on Special Transportation," next chapter.) If a child nevertheless runs off without making his bed, we should leave the bed as it is. When the child comes home he is told — without lectures or scolding — "You left your bed unmade this morning. Take care of it now please."

## Coping With Disorderliness

Teaching habits of orderliness is perhaps the one area where parents experience the greatest frustration. How is it that parents who themselves provide a model of neatness encounter such difficulty instilling this trait in their children? We can best understand this problem by tracing its roots.

In teaching the child to be orderly, our aim should be that he develop a love of orderliness that will motivate him to be neat on his own. Such an attitude can best develop if the parents proceed calmly and with patience, and without exaggerated expectations. Parents who lack such tolerance are apt to nag and scold the child, who then becomes resentful and hardly disposed to value tidiness. Thus the attempt degenerates into a futile and never-ending struggle.

Many parents find it particularly hard to moderate their expectations, especially if they have believed for years that they cannot stand disorder. They may tell themselves again and again, "I shouldn't make such a fuss — I shouldn't get so angry when the kids leave their things all over — but I just can't stand the mess!" As long as parents demand inwardly that things always be neat, they will continue to have trouble maintaining the self-control necessary to effectively train their children in neatness. Mothers who drive themselves to keep their houses constantly in order can expect only frayed nerves and unhappy children.

The parents' anger is often intensified because they view their children's disorder as evidence of their own failure — "What kind of mother am I that I can't get my kids to keep their room in order?" Parents who know they have this problem can tell themselves, "It's true that I haven't yet succeeded in teaching my children orderliness. However, that doesn't make *me* a failure." When parents realize that they do not have to think in terms of "failure" or lack of self-worth, they will find it much easier to cope with their anger.

Some parents also begin to worry about the children's character — "What's going to be with these kids if they're so careless and disorderly now?" This, too, contributes nothing to solving the problem in the present.

It may help to consider the matter from the child's point of view. The child has not developed the habit of putting things in their place. He knows he *should*, but he hates to; he'd much rather read or play some game. So, he puts it off. In this way more and more items accumulate — until the room is in such a state that the last thing he wants to do is clean it up.

The more someone tells him what a slob he is, and how he doesn't care at all about the mess in his room, the more he comes to believe it. His reaction then is: "Okay, so I'm a slob — so I don't care what my room is like. That's the way I am." He may still be blaming himself for being this way, but he does nothing about it.

Caught in a cycle like this — often for years — parents sometimes become so weary of the entire ordeal that they finally give up, telling themselves, "All right, it's his room. Let him keep it as messy as he likes." This may relieve some of the tension, but it is obviously no solution. Besides, maintaining such an "I don't care" attitude is difficult; sooner or later, parents usually go back to getting angry at the disorder.

If they wish to succeed in changing their children's disorderly habits, parents must first learn to control their anger. This means refraining from sarcastic remarks such as "It's no wonder you can't find your notebook in this mess." It means they must practice telling themselves — instead of "Those miserable slobs! I can't stand their messes anymore! They don't care about *me* at all!" — "I don't particularly like this mess but I *can* tolerate it. Besides, getting angry over it just makes me miserable and doesn't get me anywhere. They just have bad habits, and I'll have to patiently teach them better ones."

To make a fresh start, a conference is called, and the subject of orderliness brought up. After a discussion on the importance and advantages of neatness during which the children contribute their ideas (pleasure it gives us, easier to find things, helps us function better), the mother says, "From now on we're going to set aside fifteen minutes every day before supper for straightening up the room. I'll remind you, and be around to give you a hand too."

This should be seen as a period of training. Developing new habits takes time. We must start at (or return to) the beginning, showing the children how to straighten up their room and helping them with it. Little by little we can withdraw from the enterprise leaving them to do the job by themselves.

Parents should be careful, as they assist the child, to refrain from any critical comments such as "Look at the way this room looks! Books all over, clothes lying around . . . and what's this junk doing on your desk?" A pleasant atmosphere should surround this activity. For example, if we come in at the arranged time and find one child busy with a book instead of cleaning up, we very calmly take it from him, take him by the hand and say, in a friendly way, "Come, let's start cleaning up."

Don't start putting things away as the child watches, expecting him to join in. Better to ask: "All right — what would you like me to help you with?" Surprisingly, when they see our willingness to help them, children will quite often tell us, "It's okay Mom, we can do it by ourselves."

A child can be taught, when he thinks he is finished, to

stand at the door and survey the room to make sure everything is in order. One can prepare a checklist for him, including, for instance:

1. Books and games put away
2. Desk tidied
3. Floor cleaned up

Remember to praise the child's efforts.

A few minutes should also be set aside before bedtime, after the children are in pajamas, for bringing dirty clothes to the hamper and preparing fresh clothing for the next morning. All this is done together with them. The problem of dirty laundry can sometimes be solved by hanging a colorful pillowcase with a loop sewn onto it on the back of the closet or bedroom door.

If the child persists, for instance, in dropping his clothes all over the room and leaving them there, we might try applying some logical consequences. All clothes lying on his bed will not be washed (this may mean no clean shirt for Shabbath). By the time several days' clothing has piled up, the child may be so bothered by the mess that he decides it is better to put his things away. One mother who tried this with her nine-year-old son reported that one such experience was enough to rid the boy of his habit.

Disorder in a teen-ager's room requires special handling. Keep in mind that such a long-standing bad habit cannot be changed easily. The youngster needs our encouragement to help him get over his negative attitude toward cleaning up. In a pleasant talk, we might say to him, "I know how you hate to clean up and how hard it is for you to bring yourself to do it. But you know, there are times when I don't feel so much like cleaning up either — I just have to push myself to do it. Afterwards, I feel good. The trick is not to think about what an awful job cleaning up is but to just push yourself to do it. Afterwards when you're finished, you realize it wasn't so bad after all. Then instead of having to look at the mess and feel disgusted with yourself because of your lazy habits, you'll have the pleasure of an orderly room where everything can be easily found. And you'll feel good about having succeeded in pushing yourself to do the job." We should offer the youngster our help if he wants it, getting him started with a general reorganization of the room, showing him how to keep small items in boxes and so on.

The teen-ager should be reminded — but not more than once a day — to straighten up his room. If this is done pleasantly, without complaints or criticism, he will generally make some effort. If the room is then still in bad shape, we should be specific about what remains to be done. For example, "Your clothes need to be hung up, your desk still has to be tidied, and the papers on the floor have to be picked up." A nice way to call this to the youngster's attention is to post a small notice on the door (or, if there is one, on the bulletin board) with a list of the remaining tasks. If the room is in fairly good shape you might write, "The room looks good except for..." Don't allow yourself to start thinking, "I shouldn't have to tell him all this — he knows it." The fact is, if we don't tell him, he won't do it. We might as well accept this and not disturb ourselves with thinking about how things *should* be.

There is no harm done, however, if we at times tell an older child that it upsets us to see disorder in his room. With this we let him know that even if a messy room doesn't bother him, he should keep it neat out of consideration for us. Naturally, this should not be said in an excited or angry tone of voice, as this would convey intolerance.

We have to keep in mind, though, that as much as children may want to please us, they may be loath to make the necessary effort. Typically, they will answer "Yes Mom," yet still make little effort to improve to get their room neater. In this case, we might ask for some assurance — for example, "I'd feel better if I could have some kind of commitment from you, like 'Mom, we'll really try to keep the room in better shape from now on.'"

## CARELESSNESS

Practically all children occasionally leave items such as books and jackets lying around. It is best to calmly tell the child, for example, "You left your briefcase in the hall." Or, one can call the child in and say, "Take a look and see what has to be put away." If the child's things were left in the kitchen we can tell him, "I can't work here with these things lying around." Discussions can be helpful too; for example, "Kids, there's a problem with the books left lying around the living room after Shabbath. What shall we do?"

However, when children habitually leave their belongings strewn about causing perpetual disorder in the house, more drastic measures may be called for. The mother may have to call the children together and tell them, "Kids, it's unpleasant to have to ask you to put your things away.On the other hand, I don't want to be putting them away for you either. So from now on, when I find your things, I'll be putting them in this bag." The children should be shown where the bag (or box, if preferred) will be kept — perhaps hung in the kitchen closet, or in some out-of-the-way place so that the children experience maximum unpleasant consequences from their messiness. Sometimes a shelf can be allotted for quick clearance of items left lying around; even the top of the refrigerator can be used. All this must be done quietly and pleasantly; the method loses much of its effectiveness if we start off, for example, by saying, "I'm going to teach you kids not to leave your stuff all over the house!"

Children frequently have a habit of leaving clothing and towels lying around the bathroom. It is best to quietly call the child in and, with a slight gesture of the hand, tell him very simply, "Look." No more words are necessary; the child will catch the hint and know what to do. A discussion about the situation may be appropriate, but at some other time.

Humorous notes can be used from time to time. A note pinned to a pair of carelessly thrown pajamas such as "How I long to be under the pillow!" or one taped to the uncapped toothpaste tube that says "I like to be in the cabinet with my cover on" can often convey our message more effectively than spoken words. Other amusing and novel ways of handling problems of disorderliness can be thought up. For instance, if books are left lying around, we can hand a child a pile of them and say, "Here — you just became a librarian."

Children who frequently mislay their things should not be assisted in finding them. If a child comes to us complaining "I can't find my notebook," we should merely respond "I'm awfully sorry," refraining from any lectures. In this way he may learn to put things away more carefully. To foster greater responsibility, a child can be required to pay for replacements of lost school equipment from his own savings or pocket money, if he has any. In the case of lost sweaters, jackets, boots, or briefcases, the child should at least contribute toward the purchase of new items. Replacing a lost sweater or jacket with a worn-out hand-me-down can be a good punishing consequence. The fewer words said about this, the better. The child is usually sufficiently self-critical over his carelessness and does not need any admonishment from us. It is a good idea to label all articles which could get lost with the child's name.

## A FINAL WORD

Because mothers are usually more directly involved with maintaining order, they are the ones to speak to the children most often about it. As a result, children sometimes get the idea that order isn't really so crucial since it seems to matter to only one parent. Therefore, it is important that the father join the mother in stressing the need for maintaining neat rooms and an orderly house in general.

## Cleanliness and Appearance

When our sages depict a ladder leading to perfection of character, they list cleanliness as the fourth rung.[5] Just as royal statues are washed daily, so must we, who are created in God's image, keep our bodies clean.[6] Cleanliness is even considered an aspect of holiness.[7]

In teaching cleanliness to their children, parents should try to be tolerant and relaxed. It is unreasonable to expect a child to be constantly clean, and a mother who insists on this is likely to wear out both herself and the child. What very often prompts the mother is concern over what others will think of her. Once she is aware of this, she can work on reducing her dependence on the approval of other people.

On the other hand, children need not be sloppily dressed. To remind a child about his appearance, parents can give cues such as "Take a look and see what you need to do with your shirt." This is more effective than constant reminders to "tuck that shirt in."

For children who don't like washing their hands, a dab of hand cream every time they have done so can serve as an incentive. Try to keep washing routines cheerful; avoid statements such as "How did you get yourself so dirty?" or "Get those filthy hands washed right away!" An older child can be told in a friendly and matter-of-fact way to wash his hands; a younger child can be lead to the sink as we say "Come, your hands need to be washed." It pays to be patient and not push the child to get himself clean in a hurry. We may get a little less done, but the reward, in terms of developing a positive attitude toward cleanliness, is well worth it.

A sturdy stepstool kept next to the sink encourages self-help. Likewise, a small mirror at child height helps develop good habits. Towel hooks should be low, and strong loops sewn to hand towels to keep these on their hooks.

# Getting Up and Bedtime Routines

## Morning Routines

Mornings are a time of tension in many homes. Many parents nervously rush their children through the morning routines: "Come on, get up!" "Stop dawdling and get dressed!" "Get going or you'll be late for school!" "Hurry up, eat your breakfast!" By the time the last child is safely out the door and on his way to school, parents often feel ready to collapse. What's to be done?

The main problem seems to be that we've taken over for the child. By rushing him, we make him think his getting to school on time is our responsibility. So he starts to rely on us, becoming lax himself. If we want the child to take charge instead, we have to step back and allow some natural consequences to take their course.

This means, first of all, maintaining a pleasant, relaxed atmosphere in the house each morning. It is amazing, once we've stopped trying to run the show, how quickly children catch on and begin to assume responsibility themselves. As these mothers report:

In the mornings I used to nag my son constantly in order to get him to school on time. Following a discussion in the group, I decided that perhaps he was old enough and could be made responsible for going on time without my nagging.

I didn't discuss this with him or do anything. Every fifteen or twenty minutes I would nicely tell him the time (he can't read the clock as yet); and after a few days he caught on that it was up to him to stop dawdling and get out on time. Still, this was not so easy for him and at first, he would often come to school five or ten minutes late. Now, a few weeks later, he's almost never late.

My kids were very busy when they woke up in the morning, coloring, playing, talking — they absolutely never thought of getting dressed. I was always saying, get up, get dressed, it's late. I hated doing it, but always ended up doing it anyway.

Finally I made up my mind, no more. It's their job to go to school and get there on time. I managed with nearly one hundred percent success to stop nagging. But they, as usual, were coloring, talking, and playing — while I was relaxing and wondering what would happen. To my great surprise, at a certain point, they looked at their watches and when they realized how late it was, began to rush like mad. I still catch myself hoping they'll get to school late, to teach them not to dawdle — but it doesn't happen!

A little planning and organization will also help. If we take out time in the evening to lay out clothing for the next day, prepare lunches, and get briefcases ready for school, there is that much less to do in the morning when time is at a premium. This is especially important when there is a baby to care for as well. Needless to say, getting up early enough can make all the difference.

## GETTING CHILDREN OUT OF BED

If possible, give the children their own alarm clock; that way you won't have to wake them up. If you are the one to wake them up in the morning, do it pleasantly. Pull up the shades and in a friendly manner announce, "Time to get up." Some children can rouse themselves quickly; others need a couple of minutes to get used to the idea. With a child who has particular difficulty, it helps if we commiserate — "I know — it's so hard to get up in the morning." There is nothing wrong with giving a reminder, but don't go into the room repeatedly to urge the child out of bed.

## MAKING BEDS

As discussed in Chapter 8, children should be required, once they become capable, to make their beds. A good rule is "BBB" — beds before breakfast. In other words, a child does not get breakfast until he has made his bed.

## DRESSING THE YOUNG CHILD

Nursery-school age children who are as yet unable to dress themselves will often resist us as we try to dress them. A good way to handle this is to leave the child alone and tell him that when he is ready to be dressed, he should call. If the child seems not to care, preferring to stay in pajamas, inform him that children who are not dressed cannot come to breakfast. This usually does the trick.

## TEACHING CHILDREN TO DRESS THEMSELVES

The child's first efforts at self-dressing are rather clumsy. It seems to take him forever to get each piece of clothing on. We may be tempted to jump in and quickly do the job for him. However, if we can remain patient during this period, letting the child do what he can and helping him with the rest, it will prove worth it in the long run.

149

The better the child gets at dressing himself, the more you should withdraw to let him handle it on his own. You can say, "Here are your clothes. Whenever you can't manage call me and I'll help you." The child, however, may still want you to stay with him; in this case you can divide things up. For example: "You put on your underpants and I'll do the shirt," "You do one shoe and I'll do the other."

The fact that a child has learned to dress himself does not mean that he always wants to do it. He may tell you "I can't get my shirt on" when he really can do it quite easily. It's best to answer, "I know you'd like me to help you but I think you can do it." Of course, all children like a bit of "babying" now and then and we should be willing to help them with dressing occasionally even when they don't really need it.

## CHOOSING CLOTHING

While older children should, in general, be allowed to decide for themselves what to wear, it is probably better to put a younger child's clothes out for him. If the child wants to wear something else, you can respect the request assuming it is reasonable.

Sometimes an older child will have trouble deciding what to put on in the morning. He will often turn down suggestions from the parent as well. Here an empathic response is best: "I know — it's so hard to decide"; then leave the child alone.

There is no need for arguments about putting on a sweater. Send the child out to check the weather, or the outdoor thermometer if you have one, and then let him decide. If he is uncomfortable for a day because of an inappropriate choice, he'll learn from that experience. If, however, you're worried that the child will catch cold, insist that he put on a sweater even if he doesn't want to. You can avoid arguments by not responding to his protests but answering simply, "I know, but please put the sweater on anyway."

Yet another alternative is to hand the child his sweater

and say, "Here, put this in your briefcase so you'll have it in case you're cold."

## TIMERS AS AIDS

A kitchen timer is useful for discouraging dawdling in young children who cannot yet tell time. Set the timer for when they have to be finished dressing and teach them to check it now and then. You can make a game out of being dressed before the bell rings. The timer can also remind children how much time remains for eating breakfast or before they have to leave the house.

## WHEN THE CHILD IS LATE

If it appears that the child may be late for school, do nothing. Allow him to be late and experience the teacher's displeasure. Don't write him any excuse notes. If the teacher is permissive about lateness, you might write a note asking him or her to apply some punishing consequences.

This does not mean, of course, that you are unconcerned. You should explain to the child that punctuality is a virtue and that it is important that he be in school on time. But it is his responsibility, not yours.

What about breakfast? We can save ourselves much unnecessary annoyance by leaving it up to the child how much breakfast he wants. If he decides to eat a skimpy breakfast or none at all because he is running late, don't be too concerned about it. True, food is important, and some mothers find it very difficult to send a child off to school hungry, seeing this as neglect of their duty. What, though, is really worse for the child: to go a little hungry, or to be subjected to an hour of nagging every morning? It becomes easier to deal with our feelings of compassion when we view the situation from this perspective.

## WHEN THE CHILD RELIES ON
## SPECIAL TRANSPORTATION

We don't have to nervously rush the child to make it on time for the school bus or car pool. Instead, we can try setting the timer and telling him that if he isn't finished dressing when it rings, we will have to do the rest for him. If he isn't ready when the timer goes off, go in and stuff him rather unceremoniously (but not angrily) into the rest of his clothes. (If he is actually still in bed, pull him out at this point.) Try to make your dressing him sufficiently unpleasant so that he will not be eager to have you do it again.

Another way of handling the problem is to offer the child some kind of incentive. Set the timer for a specified period — say, fifteen minutes. Explain to him that if he has all his clothes on before the bell rings, he gets some small reward such as a special sandwich spread for lunch. If the bell rings and he hasn't made it, you'll still put his clothes on him but he won't get the special treat.

## Bedtime Routines

Toward evening, most of us begin to look forward to that wonderful hour when our children are in bed and we can have a little time to ourselves. Much as we may want some peace and quiet, however, we need to avoid becoming anxious over it and telling ourselves, "I've got to get those kids into bed! I must have some rest or I'll surely collapse!" When we are nervous about getting our children to bed, we inevitably show it by our irritable way of talking to them; the children are then more likely to resist our efforts.

We need to view the situation more calmly. Even if the "worst" happened and the children were all still up hours after their bedtime, we would still be able to cope. Instead of anticipating possible difficulties as some sort of catastrophe, we can think to ourselves, "Even if I don't get the kids to bed on time, I'll still be okay. I'll survive." When we then proceed getting the children to bed without so much anxiety, we will be more likely to gain their cooperation.

## GETTING YOUNGER CHILDREN READY FOR BED

Allow plenty of time for the bedtime procedure, starting the children right after supper. Try to be relaxed, leading them pleasantly through the various routines, so that it can be enjoyable for both you and them. Try to spend a moment or two with each child as you tuck him into bed and say the *Shema'* with him; then give him a hug and kiss, turn out the lights and leave.

If a child now comes out and asks for some drink or snack, tell him very pleasantly that he can have these in the morning. (One can remind children before putting them to bed to take drinks if they are thirsty, as there will be no coming out later to ask for them.) Whatever reason he comes out for, don't make yourself angry by thinking "Why can't he stay in bed!" Instead, lead the child calmly yet firmly back to bed right away. When children call us to come, we can go in and quietly explain that now is their time to go to sleep. It reassures the child if we tell him where we will be, and say we will look in on him very soon. Children who no longer need toileting help may be told that if they have to go to the bathroom, they should go quietly without calling us.

## BEDTIME ROUTINES FOR OLDER CHILDREN

As children get older, they will no longer require your close supervision. Let them know when to start getting ready for bed, then check up on them from time to time, keeping reminders to a minimum. Timers can be useful for signaling when to get out of the bathtub, or how much time is left for playing until the child has to be in bed. If the child ignores the bell, we can say, "The bell rang — you know what that means."

Instead of the usual nightly reminders — "Don't forget to

153

brush your teeth" or "Did you brush your teeth?" — try hanging up this sign in the bathroom:

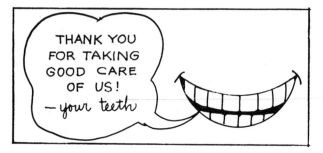

A pleasant way to remind a child about brushing his teeth is to ask, "Did you . . . ?" as we gesture with our finger across our teeth.

## HANDLING RESISTANCE

It is best not to argue with children about their bedtime. If a child says he doesn't want to go to sleep, or asks to stay up to finish reading a book or play some game, tell him, "I'm sorry honey, but now is your bedtime."

With a child who regularly grumbles or makes a face when asked to get ready for bed, a quiet talk can be helpful. You might say to him, "I know how much you don't like going to bed at night. But you need your sleep — I can't let you stay up until all hours of the night. Try to be sensible about it, won't you?"

Sometimes a child will be more cooperative if you decide together with him on a bedtime which he then commits himself to stick to.

## INCENTIVES

A small incentive can sometimes help tremendously to get children into bed on time. In one family, those who have put on pajamas, brushed their teeth, and are ready for bed on time can play in their rooms for an extra half hour. It works like magic, reports the mother.

 Jealousy

A certain amount of jealousy among children is normal and we should not be overly concerned about it, nor invest too much effort trying to prevent it. Parents are often unaware that excessive concern about jealousy makes them act in ways that actually increase it. For instance, a mother, in cutting a cake, will try hard to make each piece exactly the same, hoping it will put an end to the children's eyeing of each other's pieces to make sure no one got more. But the children now hover over the mother as she divides the cake, scrutinizing each piece even more carefully than before. The more we try to prevent apparent discrimination, the more vigilant children become.

The best thing we can do to prevent jealousy is not to worry about it. Most children experience some jealousy at one time or another; if no one pays much attention to it, they generally get over it on their own.

## Jealousy of a New Baby

Much has been written about the jealousy of the "dethroned" oldest child. At first, the explanation goes, he is an only child, enjoying the exclusive attention of his parents. Then suddenly he is ousted from this special position by a small intruder; as an

155

inevitable result, he feels jealous. Of course, many older children do indeed experience such feelings toward the new baby; yet we need not assume that this is necessarily true for all children.

The important thing is not to be constantly on the alert, looking for signs of jealousy. If they do appear, they are normal and are no cause for alarm. Parents should not make the mistake of going to special lengths to appease the older child's jealousy, such as giving in to his demands while holding the baby, or hurriedly putting the baby down when he seeks attention; this strongly encourages further demandingness in the older child. Don't hesitate to freely show affection for the new baby, and don't feel you must give the older child a hug too every time you give the baby one.

Parents can help the older child develop a positive attitude toward the baby by giving him plenty of opportunities to assist in his care, praising him liberally for any help. Children naturally sense the new baby's helplessness, and it makes them feel protective and want to do things for him. The older child can fetch a bottle or a diaper, or even assist with feeding or dressing the baby. When he asks to hold the baby, we can seat him on a carpeted floor to ensure safety.

Fortunately, the average new baby sleeps much of the time in his early months and, except for purely physical care, does not require our attention. Thus we can give most of it to the older child, helping him gradually get used to sharing it with the baby.

If the older child is to be moved to a big bed to make room for the baby, it is well to do this several months in advance; otherwise the older child may come to resent the baby for pushing him out of his place. Also, if he is to go to nursery school, have him start a couple of months beforehand so that he does not get the feeling he is being sent from the house because of the baby.

To prevent the older child from disturbing you while you feed the baby, have some toys nearby to keep him busy. One mother of several young children reads to the older ones during this time. Before settling down with the baby she tells them, "Get your toys and books — we have our time together now." Of course when there are older children around they can be asked to occupy the little ones; you can then enjoy the luxury of being all alone with the baby.

Often a child will react to a baby's arrival by wishing he too could be a baby again. He will ask for a bottle or a pacifier, or revert to other outgrown behavior. Such temporary regression is no cause for alarm. Parents can humor the child's desire to be a baby to a certain extent, while at the same time emphasizing to him the advantages of being grown-up. If he wants to drink from a bottle for a while, let him; he is unlikely to want it for long. He will discover that the milk's flow is disappointingly slow, and that the bottle isn't at all the great experience he thought it would be. As for a pacifier, since prolonged use can damage the teeth, it is better to let the child have one at bedtime only. We can remove the pacifier after the child has fallen asleep, explaining to him beforehand why we are doing this.

At times, the older child may show his jealousy with suspicious hugs that make the baby cry. It is essential that we not suspect the child of deliberately wanting to hurt the baby; assume rather that it is a clumsy expression of affection. Thus, rather than calling out "You're hurting the baby!" tell him, "Hug the baby gently." You can explain: "You're so big and strong; you don't realize when you hug the baby that it hurts — that's why he cries. Let me show you how to hug him" (model on child). "Now let's see how gently you can hug him."

The same goes for when you notice the older child playing too roughly with the baby. Take the child's hand in yours and say, "The baby is delicate — we have to treat him gently. If we're too rough it hurts him." Then, with your other hand, gently stroke the child's face and hand as you say, "See — this feels nice. Now let's do it to the baby." With the child's hand, softly stroke the baby on his face and hands as you say, "See —

157

the baby likes that. It feels nice. Now you do it." After letting him do it alone, praise him for it and hug him.

Physical attacks on the baby cannot, of course, be tolerated. We should immediately remove the child as we tell him quietly but firmly, "I cannot let you be with the baby if you hurt him." The child should be kept in another part of the house for a while. It is important not to scold or shame him, as this may well heighten any existing feelings of hostility toward the baby.

## Jealousy Between Older Children

Obviously, conspicuous playing of favorites by parents, especially between children close in age, can be harmful. The Talmud points up the dire outcome of Jacob's singling out of Joseph for preferential treatment:

> One should never treat one child differently than the others, since for a weight of two *sela'im* of wool that Jacob gave to his son Joseph more than to his other sons, the brothers envied him and as a result, our forefathers were forced to go down to Egypt.[1]

While there is always bound to be some jealousy, parents can keep it to a minimum by avoiding comparisons between siblings. One should never say to a child, "Why can't you be like your brother (sister)?" Try not to praise one child or extol his achievements in front of the others when there is reason to believe that it could create jealousy. When a child is jealous of a more clever or gifted sibling, don't try to talk him out of his feelings by saying for example, "Never mind if you're not so smart — you're good in sports." Rather, show understanding — "I know — you wish you could get high marks like your sister."

We can teach older children that jealousy is a bad character trait. It causes harm to others, but most of all to the person who has the trait himself. We can stress that jealousy, though it seems outwardly directed, is actually a cause of unhappiness mainly for the jealous person himself, as he needlessly torments himself with longing for others' possessions or talents.

A younger child may envy the privileges of an older one, such as a later bedtime. An empathic response such as "I know, but your bedtime is now" usually avoids arguments and helps the child accept the situation.

At the same time, we must realize that it is neither feasible nor desirable to strive to treat all our children with complete equality. We should keep this in mind when a child accuses us of favoring a sibling.

For example, eight-year-old Sarah gets a new knapsack because hers is worn out. Her older sister Miriam complains, "It's not fair! She doesn't take care of her knapsack and gets a new one, and I don't get one!" In general, we should resist the temptation of trying to reason with the child. Instead, we should show empathy. Here, rather than answering "But look, yours is in perfectly good condition — you don't need a new one!" we might commiserate with the jealous sister: "I know, you'd like to have a new one too. But look honey, you don't really need one." Surprisingly, this is usually enough to help the child get over his unhappiness and be accepting of the situation. Sometimes we might simply respond, with a friendly smile, "That's how it is." Certainly one should never tell a child, "You don't have to have everything he has!"; this only makes the child more unhappy and does nothing to reduce his jealousy. It's also best to avoid trying to balance things out — for instance, it would not be a good idea to promise to buy the older girl a new pencil case.

Remember, the child cries "unfair!" in the hope that it will weaken our stand, enabling him to get what he wants. Don't let him draw you into a defense of your position. Don't try to prove that you really are fair. And be sure not to let yourself become angry over the unfairness of *his* accusations!

All this is not to say that a child's complaints are never justified. If, after thinking things over, we decide that they are, we should do our best to rectify the situation. But even then our response to the child must be without guilt or apology. Whether he is justified in his complaint or not, our answer need consist of no more than a gentle "We try our best to treat all of you fairly."

A child will sometimes accuse the parent of loving another child more than him. Here too an empathic response is best. Criticism such as "Why are you so jealous?" only reinforces the jealousy. Attempts to reassure the child by telling him, "You have no reason to be jealous — you know that we love all our children equally" are generally not helpful either. The parent should listen attentively to the child, responding initially by reflecting his feelings: "You seem to feel that I love your brother (sister) more than you. Let me tell you something. I have a big heart with room for love for every one of you. I love each and every one of my children."

Just as we cannot hope to treat all our children with complete equality, so is it virtually impossible, much as we might wish, to love them exactly the same. It may be painful to recognize this, but we might as well face it — some children are just easier to love. We readily feel affection for the agreeably behaved child, or for the youngster with a friendly and outgoing nature. We should not react with guilt if we find that we have trouble feeling affection for a particularly difficult child. Rather, we should see it as a challenge to truly love this child as well.

## PROBLEMS AT MEALTIME

Mealtimes are frequently the setting for a chorus of "It's not fair!" and "She got more than me!" Don't upset yourself by thinking how awful it is that your children display such bad character traits; try, instead, to see it all as a little funny. Refrain from responses such as "Oh stop it, it doesn't matter!"

Instead you might answer in a humorous vein, "So you don't want yours?"

Later, you can have a talk with the children. You might start by saying, "Suppose you are sitting alone at the table and you get a piece of cake. Would you be happy?" The children will no doubt answer yes. "But now, someone else is at the table and he also got cake, and you notice that his piece is bigger. Suddenly you're unhappy with the same piece of cake that you were happy with before. Tell me, what would you have to do so you would be happy again?" Someone is likely to give the logical answer; if not, you give it — "Just don't look at the other person's piece to see if it's bigger. You see, then you're happy."

Now, when there is complaining again in the future, you need only remind the children, "Remember what we said about not looking to see if someone else got more?"

Another method was presented by a mother who found that it put a quick end to her children's complaining. When they carried on about someone getting more, she simply told them, "Whoever complains, I'll take some away."

If children are screaming all at once — "I want first!" "Give me first!" "It's not fair that he always gets first!" — simply ignore the carrying on and refuse to give out any food until there is quiet.

 Fighting

None of us likes to see our children fight. As the Psalmist describes it: "How good and pleasant it is when siblings dwell together in harmony."[1] Yet, inevitably, children will fight with each other; most commonly because of competition, jealousy, or disputes over the possession of some object or over who must do a particular task.

The dynamics of a fight are fairly simple. One child does or says something which the other regards as objectionable. The second child then responds with verbal or physical abuse, the first child escalates the hostilities with further responses, and so on.

Parents differ in their reactions to the fighting. Some try to settle their children's fights for them by playing judge. After a lengthy investigation they decide who is right and who is wrong; Mr. Wrong then gets scolded or punished. What happens then? Mr. Right says to himself, "Hah hah! He got it! Mommy says he's wrong!" And Mr. Wrong ends up mad, both at mother and at Mr. Right. All we do is set the scene for the next battle. This approach also greatly encourages the children to involve the parents in their fights, with each child trying to get the parent to side with him.

Some parents react by preaching to their children. "You're

the older one — you should know better!" "You children should love each other and not fight." Such words, however, are usually wasted. Children who fight are angry at each other and in no mood for lectures.

Another way of handling the fighting, generally not too effective, is to send back messages when one of the quarreling children comes to complain:

> David: Uri won't let me play with the fire truck!
> Mother: Tell him he has to let you play with it.
>
> Rachel: Mommy, Shulamith hit me!
> Mother: Tell her that's not nice.

Or, the parent may go in to personally reprimand the offending party. For instance, seven-year-old Shoshanah comes to tell mother that five-year-old Yoni won't let her write and keeps pulling away her pencil and paper. Mother goes in to take the younger brother to task: "Stop bothering your sister — do you hear!" The problem, though, with this approach is that while the one child may really be bothering the other, we never know whether the "victim" may not have provoked the aggressive behavior he complains of in the first place, perhaps to have the satisfaction of seeing the other one get it while he glories in his innocence. We should not forget also that children have scores to settle with each other, and that the younger brother, in this case, may well be getting back at his older sister for something she did to him the day before.

But victims are not always treated with kid gloves either. They may be told, when they come to complain, "He wouldn't hit you for nothing. Come on — what did you do to him?" Unfortunately, the child thus accused feels bitter and is likely to go back to try to settle the score on his own.

In some situations parents will attempt arbitration. They will try, for example, to persuade one child that the other didn't intend to be mean or hurt him. However, the victim of abuse is usually left unconvinced and parents often end up in an unpleasant argument. Attempts to make peace *during* a fight are especially unlikely to work.

Sometimes, when they feel they can't take it anymore — when it seems like they've heard nothing all day but "He hit me!" "No, she started it!" "He took my toy away!" "Mommy, she called me a pest!" — the parents' exasperation gives way to anger and screaming. "I can't stand another minute of this dreadful fighting! Stop it now — do you hear!" Often they will end up spanking both children, yelling, "I don't care who started — you're both getting it!" While such reactions of anger and violence may make the parents feel better for the moment, they hardly encourage the peaceful resolution of conflict which the parents want the children to learn.

## Staying Calm

If we wish to handle the problem effectively, we must resolve first not to become aggravated over the fighting or let it make us angry. As fervently as we may want peace, we had better accept the fact that for the time being at least, there is going to be fighting: an unfortunate reality, certainly unpleasant, but not "horrible" or "unbearable."

Parents have to avoid blaming or judging their children ("Why is he so mean to her!" "Why can't she let her have the toy!"), even if only to themselves. They must think in terms of how to best influence the children to get along better with each other. This calls for an objective and non-judgmental attitude.

Parents should also avoid blaming themselves for their children's fighting ("What am *I* doing wrong that they fight so much!"). The parents' assumption here seems to be that if they did everything right, their children would never fight. Aside from this being a rather unrealistic demand, parents should realize that, even were they to do everything perfectly, their children would still probably fight. Squabbling and quarreling between children is so normal that there is practically no family that is free of it. When parents no longer see themselves as personally responsible for their children's fights and stop viewing each conflict as if *they* should have prevented it, they will find themselves much better able to stay calm enough to handle the problem effectively.

While an unusual amount of fighting may be cause for concern, dwelling on thoughts such as "When will they ever learn to get along?" and "How will I be able to continue coping if this keeps up?" will only make us anxious; it is best therefore to put these out of our minds completely.

## Staying Out of Fights

Next, as difficult as this may be, we must learn to refrain as far as possible from interfering to settle our children's fights. True, it is our responsibility to teach our children not to fight; however, this cannot be accomplished by our intervening while any fighting is going on. We must find another time for working out with the children the ways and means of settling their difficulties peacefully. Might not one child take unfair advantage of another child when we remove ourselves in this way? Perhaps. But we cannot hope to supervise matters so as to make everything always completely fair; we might as well give up the effort.

It takes some self-control, for example, to watch a little one getting her toys snatched away and her hair pulled and not interfere; but we have to keep in mind that we cannot always be around to protect our children. They are bound, sooner or later, to be exposed to others who will not always be kind to them; they may as well get used to some rough treatment and learn to tolerate it.

If we have until now tried to settle their fights for them, we should explain to the children that we will no longer interfere because we want them to learn to resolve their own conflicts. Now when we hear the usual agitated voices, we resist the urge to run in to see what happened, instead calmly going about our business as usual. (Haven't we seen how those ear-piercing screams are often nothing more than acts which the child puts on for our benefit — just to get us to come running, and, at the same time, powerfully impress us with how horribly he is being treated so as to get our protection as the victim!) When someone comes to complain, for instance, "It's not fair — he's always starting up!" or when a child runs in crying, "She called me stupid and said she'd tell her friends not to play with me!" we tell him, "I'm really sorry that you're fighting. See if you can find a peaceful way to settle it by yourselves," or, "I have confidence that you can settle this quietly." The children must not conclude that we have suddenly become indifferent to the fighting. Quite the contrary, we care very much; but for the good of all we no longer mix in. Responses such as "I'm not getting into this — you kids have to settle it by yourselves" should be avoided as these sound uncaring.

Parents usually experience a great sense of relief when they no longer feel responsible for resolving their children's conflicts. Though they should not expect any sudden decrease in the incidence of fighting, parents will find that their children actually begin to settle conflicts by themselves. Here are two examples:

I was a bit skeptical when our group leader advised us not to mix in when the children fight. But the incident that followed proved to me that she was right. I was lying in my bed hearing my two girls, six and seven, having a fight over a doll, the older one saying nasty words to the younger one. From my bed I listened and got upset, feeling the older one was wrong and thinking I have to teach them to be fair and talk nicely to each other. Their words grew louder and I grew angrier. The only thing that prevented me from yelling from my bed was the fact that the baby was sleeping right next to me. Then the older one hit the younger one and the younger one began crying. I was ready to jump out of my bed but hesitated for a minute. It was worth while waiting. Hearing her younger sister crying, the older girl felt guilty and changed her attitude. She said "I'm sorry" to her younger sister, gave her the doll they were fighting over and behaved just as I had been trying to teach her to.

My four-year-old was coloring with her markers. She warned her three-year-old brother not to touch them, threatening that if he did, she would write on him. He ignored her, and as he reached for the markers, she wrote on his arm. My three-year-old turned to me for help. When he saw that I wasn't getting involved, he got himself a stool and washed his arm off all on his own.

Fights tend also to resolve themselves more quickly when we stay out. As one mother related:

When I manage to keep myself from interfering in the children's fights, I find that, although there may not be less fights, still, the fights blow over more quickly. But most importantly, I have not become involved, upset, angry, and so on. I am not worn out as I tend to be when I do step in and then matters just go on and on.

Parents who view their children's fighting as a never-ending affair might try for one day to keep track of the actual number and duration of fights. They may be surprised to find that total fighting time is far below what they had supposed. One mother who had complained about the "constant" squabbling between her two little girls was amazed to find, when she kept a record, that there were only five brief incidents during the day, each lasting no longer than two minutes! The fighting certainly becomes easier to tolerate when we gain a truer picture of its extent.

Of course, if we have a longtime habit of settling our children's conflicts for them, we may not be able to give it up so quickly. Sometimes exasperation gets the better of us; at other times we are not strong enough to resist the children, who leave us no peace until we settle some quarrel. Staying out of fights is no easy matter. Certainly we should not be upset with ourselves if, in spite of a firm resolve not to intervene, we nevertheless find ourselves getting involved anyway.

## When to Intervene

While it is strongly recommended that parents allow children to work out their differences by themselves, this does not have to become a hard-and-fast rule. For example, a six-year-old girl gets up on her younger sister's bed while she is trying to rest and starts kicking at her with both legs. We might quietly take the older girl away as we say to her, "I don't think she likes being kicked that way." Or, two children are hurling insults at each other. They may be told rather firmly, "No name calling — it hurts other people's feelings." When a child comes to ask for help in settling some dispute, we can sometimes offer suggestions such as "Have you tried saying it nicely?" or ask him, "What do you think you could do?"

While forcing children to share toys and possessions is not a good idea, we can at times help them work out a fair system. For example, when one child comes to complain about another who won't share, we might ask, "How long does each of you want to have it?" and then suggest that the schedule be written down and posted somewhere in the room.

It is understandably difficult to ignore squabbling when it goes on under our very nose. While it is best in this case to quickly exit the scene and busy ourselves elsewhere, we can also ask the quarreling children to leave the room. One might say, for example, "Kids, please settle this elsewhere." The children may first be given a choice: "Please — either stop the quarreling or leave the room."

## PHYSICAL AGGRESSION

We can decide to ignore children who are hitting or kicking in their room, intervening to separate them only when the fighting gets rough. In this case we say to them, "I cannot let you hurt each other like this; I must separate you" and then proceed to put each child in a separate room for a cooling-off period. However, we should not ignore any attacks by one child on another that take place in our presence. Common sense also dictates that we intervene to protect babies from any onslaughts by an older child. A toddler or young child who attacks a baby should not be scolded but rather removed from the scene as we tell him quietly, "I cannot let you hurt the baby."

On the other hand, there are parents who feel that since it is wrong to hit another, children must never be permitted to do so. Thus the children are told, whenever there is any physical aggression, "You are not allowed to hit (kick) someone," and if they still do not stop they are separated as before. This does not mean, though, that we must intervene every time a child comes to tell us "(So and so) hit me!" If we didn't see what exactly happened, it might be best to simply respond, "I'm sorry — I'll talk to him about it later."

We should try to be empathic when talking to children about hitting. Statements such as "I know it was hard for you to control yourself but you're not allowed to hit him (her)" show understanding, and at the same time convey that there are limits to acceptable behavior. A child who hits a lot because "the others make me angry" can be told, "The next time someone makes you angry, don't hit. Come and tell me about it instead."

As for biting, we should keep in mind that children will

often sink their teeth into another child's arm without actually biting down. It doesn't hurt, but the other child comes to you to complain anyway. If you don't see tooth marks, you can be pretty sure that nothing much happened. The same goes for scratching. You can examine the child's arm as you say, "Hmm — it doesn't look too bad; but you can tell your brother (sister) that nails aren't for hurting people." However, if we see bad tooth marks or nail marks on anyone's arm, we should strongly reprimand the child who did it.

Sometimes parents try to teach a child not to bite, kick, or scratch by doing it to him to show him what it feels like. This, however, sets a poor example for the child. Even though we are doing it for educational purposes, we are likely only to cause resentment. A better approach is to tell the biting child, "The next time you bite, I will have to tape your mouth closed." If he then bites again, cover his mouth with a piece of cloth tape one and a half inches wide. Don't leave it on too long — a minute or two will do. Scratching can be handled by cutting the child's nails very short (so that it hurts a bit), telling him, "I am cutting your nails very short so you will not be able to scratch." If he carries on, we can tell him, "I'm sorry if it hurts you, but I cannot let you scratch."

In like fashion, we can teach children not to kick by taking their shoes off whenever they do it.

## FIGHTING IN PUBLIC AND WITH FRIENDS

Fighting in public cannot generally be ignored. Children may be warned, if they begin to fight while on the bus, in a store, or some other public place, that if they don't stop they will get punished later at home. (Since the punishment is conditional, this does not contradict the restriction against deferred punishment mentioned in Chapter 5.) Logical consequences can be used as well. For example, anyone who fights while the family is visiting with relatives stays home on the next visit. If the children quarrel on the bus while being taken to town for new shoes, they are given a choice either to stop quarreling or to go back home without the new shoes. Likewise, if children start to fight in a store they are taken out and told, "Kids, I can't let you disturb the other shoppers this way. Either you remain quiet in the store, or you will have to stay outside." Of course, we must be prepared to follow through.

It is a good idea to discuss with the children appropriate behavior on the bus before any trip. Concerning window seats or sitting next to Mommy or Daddy, we can suggest that they might switch places in the middle of the trip so that everyone gets a turn at these favorite seats.

Fighting during a car trip can be easily handled: we simply pull the car over and refuse to continue until it stops.

As for children's fights with friends, we should do our best to stay out of them. Discussions with a friend's parents about a fight should be avoided, as should efforts to defend our child or blame the other one.

When small children have friends over to play, there is often considerable fighting over toys. It is best not to interfere; we can, however, go in to comfort any child who becomes upset. If things get too rough, we should send the visitor home.

Similarly, when taking a toddler to the park, it is best to let him work out his problems with the other children by himself. If he grabs toys away from the other children and then gets hit, it may teach him not to grab toys. However, we should definitely intervene if he is getting hurt, or if he is too rough with another child. A good way to stop an attack is to simply tell the aggressor, "Hey — that hurts him!"

If your child is constantly being hit by another aggressive youngster, it might be advisable to have a talk with the child's parents about the problem. While most parents will be apologetic for the behavior of their child and try to cooperate, there are those who always take their child's side, to the point of indignation at the very idea that he does anything wrong. Sometimes it can help to teach your child to ward off attacks (see discussion on hitting in the next section); often, however, the best solution is to have him come home when aggression begins.

Mothers often find their visits to each other's homes spoiled by constant fighting between their respective children. While the mothers should try to ignore minor squabbles, no doubt they will have to intervene whenever the warfare seems to be getting out of hand. Of course, the mothers can always decide to cut their visit short.

## FIGHTING AT MEALTIMES

Fighting during meals disturbs the peace of the entire family and should not be tolerated. The quarreling children should be told, "We can't enjoy our food when there is this disturbance at the table. You have a choice to behave pleasantly or to leave the table." If the children leave and then return to the table and behave well, remember to praise them: "How nice and pleasant it is at the table now."

## Discussing Fighting

With very young children, physical aggression is rarely a serious problem; the swatting, punching, and screeching that go on generally involve disputes over toys. However, even very young children can be told that they are not allowed to hurt others, either physically or by saying things that make them feel bad. Around the age of three, we can begin to encourage sharing by suggesting, "It's nice to share our things with others," and praising the child when he does — "How nice the way you're sharing your new truck." If a child is monopolizing a toy, it is best not to try to make him share it but to gently suggest, "Why don't you give him a turn? I'm sure he'd like one." When one child comes to complain about the other's unwillingness to share, we can tell him, "I guess he wants to have it to himself for a while. Why don't you wait until he's ready to share."

At the age of five one can begin to have individual talks with the child on the subject of fighting, after tempers have calmed down and the child is ready to listen. In addition to helping him work out more peaceful solutions to differences, we need to remind the child from time to time about the Torah commandments and prohibitions which relate to fighting. Our words will carry more weight if we read the laws together with him from the original Hebrew. For those who prefer English, *Love Your Neighbor* by Rabbi Zelig Pliskin is a good source which contains the basic Torah regulations pertaining to our relationships with others.

The following is a brief summary of these laws.

1. *Hitting.* The child must know that hitting others is not allowed. Even merely raising one's hand to strike another person is forbidden.[2] However, if someone raises his hand to strike us, or is actually hitting us, we may hit him to prevent him from hurting us. It is wrong to hit back in retribution.[3]

Our child may ask us why we, the parents, are permitted to hit him. We should explain that parents are allowed to hit their children to improve their behavior.[4]

2. *Causing pain with words or action.* Parents have to teach their child that we are forbidden to do anything which causes another person suffering;[5] thus we may not call others by derogatory names or insult them.[6] This is forbidden even if the other person doesn't mind because he has gotten used to it.[7] Neither may we speak to others in a harsh or critical manner, embarrass, tease, or annoy them; this includes pestering behavior. Children should be taught the sage Hillel's rule: "What is hateful to you, don't do to your fellow," and have him picture himself in the other person's position — "Suppose you were he, and someone had said (done) that to you — how would you have felt?" Remember, however, to always say this gently.

3. *Leshon hara'.* It is important to make clear to children that telling us about a sibling's or friend's bad behavior is permitted only if it serves a constructive purpose; otherwise, it

constitutes forbidden *leshon hara'* (derogatory speech).[8] Even if a child complains about a sibling because he wants us to admonish him, he should try first to admonish him privately himself. Only if that doesn't help, or if he is certain he won't be listened to, is he allowed to tell us.[9]

On the other hand, one is not allowed to accept as definitely true any derogatory report about another person.[10] However, since it may be awkward to explain this to the child in this particular situation, it is best to tell him, "Thank you for calling this to my attention. I'll talk to your brother about this some time." Later we can explain to him why we do not automatically accept what he says.

4. *Holding a grudge or seeking revenge.* The child should know that no matter how badly someone else has wronged or insulted us, we should not take revenge or hold a grudge against him.[11] It is not our business to punish people; this has to be left to God. And, just as God forgives us when we do wrong, so should we forgive others who have mistreated us.

The story of Joseph's treatment of his brothers, who had nearly murdered him but decided at the last minute to sell him as a slave instead, can be brought as an outstanding illustration of true forgiveness. The Torah relates how the brothers came to Egypt to obtain food during the famine, and how Joseph, by now the second most powerful person in Egypt, recognized them though they did not recognize him. While outwardly he treated them gruffly, this was only to give them a chance to repent for their sin. Inwardly he felt compassion for them, and when he finally revealed himself to the brothers, his only concern was to comfort them and placate their feelings of shame over their past treatment of him.

5. *Judging charitably.* We should teach our child to fulfill his Torah obligation to judge all actions of others charitably, and to always try to see the good in others.[12] We can explain, "You know, we have to love everyone, and no matter what they do, always judge their actions favorably. Sometimes it's hard — a person acts badly toward us and we think he's bad and get

angry at him. But that's wrong. It helps us to judge another person charitably sometimes, if we see him as someone who simply hasn't learned yet to behave better. Perhaps he has problems with self-control. Or, maybe he just had a rough day." Even very young children can learn to think this way.

6. *The mitzvah of admonishment.* The child should be taught that we are not to feel hatred toward someone who has treated us badly. We have the obligation to tell him how we feel, but we must do it quietly and pleasantly.[13] If we scream at the other person, we offend him and are then ourselves guilty of wrongdoing. We must not judge another person for his wrong actions,[14] but should only point them out to him.[15] However, we should not talk to the other person while he is angry, but rather wait until he has calmed down. We must then give him a chance to explain, and if he says he is sorry we must forgive him.

Also, because there is a special obligation of "not saying that which will not be heeded," there is no mitzvah to admonish if we are sure that the other person won't listen.[16]

7. *Asking for forgiveness.* Children must learn that asking for forgiveness of others whom we have hurt is part of doing *teshuvah.*[17] We can encourage this by suggesting to a child, when we see that a particular fight has left hard feelings, "He feels bad. Go tell him you're sorry."

## HANDLING SIBLING RIVALRY

Fights often start between siblings because one is trying to show that he is better than the other — by deriding his work, or denigrating his ability. Parents should explain to the child that whatever talents and abilities a person has, they all come from God. Rather than seeing ourselves as better people because of these endowments, we should be quietly thankful that we have been thus blessed.

Often an oldest child insists that because he's the oldest, the others must all do as he says. He bosses them around, often harshly criticizing them, so that the younger children become resentful and noncompliant. Here we should explain to him that if he wants the others to listen to him, he must treat them with respect and speak to them in a way which does not hurt their feelings; they will then be much more disposed to respect and listen to him. As the Sages teach: "Who receives honor? He who honors others."[18] We can ask him to put himself in the others' position — how would he want an older brother or sister to speak to him? Then we might review an incident with the child, perhaps doing some role playing. For example, we can ask, "How could you have said that so he would have really listened to you?"

## HELPING CHILDREN DEVELOP GREATER TOLERANCE

We should try to help children pinpoint the main reason for their fights: namely, their exaggerated negative evaluations of the other person's behavior. We might tell a child, "You see, when you think to yourself how *awful* it is what the other person did, or when you tell yourself that it's *terrible* when he doesn't do what you want, what happens? You get mad and then there's a fight. So, what could you tell yourself so you wouldn't get so angry?" Try to elicit from the child answers such as "I could think that it's not so awful if he doesn't do what I want" or "I could tell myself that what he did to me wasn't really so bad." Sometimes, discussions with the child about really terrible experiences can help him develop a better perspective. Greater tolerance can also be encouraged by asking the child, "I know it's not easy, but do you think you can learn to tolerate it when he acts that way?"

Children often come home complaining bitterly about the way some other child treated them. We have to point out that, difficult as it is to avoid, relating bad things about others constitutes *leshon hara'* and is forbidden unless it serves some constructive purpose, such as alerting us to another child's dangerous behavior. It's best to tell the child, "I know you're very angry at (so and so) but you're not allowed to tell me any bad things about other people."

Many fights develop because of the child's perception of something as being unfair. We should keep in mind, of course, that what the child calls "unfair" is usually what *he* happens not to like. It is best to empathize with him at first, but then help him pinpoint the true reason for his distress — his demand that things always be fair. For example, if he comes to complain "It's not fair! I had the ball and he just grabbed it from me!" we might respond at first, "I'm so sorry." We then go on to point out, softly, "Honey, maybe if you didn't insist that everything has to be fair, you wouldn't feel so bad. You see, whenever we say 'This isn't fair!' we get ourselves upset. It's much better for us if we can simply learn to accept it."

Older children sometimes display intolerance toward younger brothers or sisters who try to copy everything they do, or bother them with silly questions. Rather than telling the older child "Don't you understand — he's just a little child — you shouldn't let it bother you," we should respond, "He so looks up to you — he thinks you know everything. So he asks you whatever he wants to know. And he wants to be just like you — so he copies everything you do. It's really an honor to you. Try to see it that way."

We might also try at times to show the child how we spoil the present by continuing to mull over some unpleasant event in the past. We can say, gently, "How do you feel when you're upset? Not so good, right? Okay, something happened which got you upset. But it's over. If you continue to be upset over it, you're suffering double. Why not forget it and be happy now?"

## WILLINGNESS TO FOREGO

We can encourage children to be willing to forego — that is, to let a sibling have what he wants or have his way — by pointing out that whenever they forego in this way, they fulfill the mitzvah of doing *chesed*. Even though they may be giving something up, the good feeling from doing the mitzvah of making someone else happy compensates for the sacrifice.

Some parents like to use a point system to encourage foregoing. Every time the child foregoes, he tells the parent about it and gets a point. When a designated number of points have accumulated (at least five), the child is entitled to some special treat or a small prize.

One can also give points for specific acts of self-control which prevent fights. For instance, a child who starts fights by grabbing things away from others can be given a point whenever he controls himself and does not grab. The youngster who stirs up trouble by teasing gets points for controlling the urge to tease. Such incentives can sometimes provide the necessary motivation to make children work harder to prevent fights. As the following story illustrates:

> The prime time for fighting among my five children was suppertime, making this a difficult hour of the day for me. Many of the fights revolved around my oldest son of ten, and although I had had several private conversations with him about the fighting, it hadn't helped.
>
> One evening as I paid particular attention to what was going on, I noticed that a great deal of the fights taking place occurred between the oldest boy and his younger sister of six. For instance, he doesn't like very cold water but she loves it. So he takes the pitcher of cold water to the faucet and adds warmer water while she carries on. She, in turn, gets on his nerves with her constant teasing.
>
> I had an idea and that evening, after the younger children were in bed, made the following proposal to my son. I would make a chart, and for each evening that he would do his best to avoid fights by, for example, ignoring his sister's teasing or forgetting about taking the chill out of the water, he would get a

point. For each point received, I would pay for development of one picture from the film in the new camera he had just received from his grandfather. The chart was to be a private matter between the two of us.

He liked the idea immediately and the next evening earned one point. The following evening he forgot about the deal, but I reminded him later and also showed him some specific example of how he could have prevented a fight. The next evening he earned another point. By the time he had earned about ten points, we began forgetting to keep track. But by then the fighting had substantially decreased, mostly because the six-year-old saw that her teasing was not getting any results.

Several weeks later we received a letter from my father, asking when he could see some pictures from his grandson's new camera. That evening I told my son that he could take the last few pictures left on the film and that we would pay for development of the entire roll. I explained that although he had recorded only ten points, he deserved the rest since he had begun to really make the effort to avoid fights, not only at suppertime but during the rest of the day too.

Parents sometimes report a problem with a child who seems to always be giving in to another, more demanding sibling. If the youngster has an easy nature and does not appear to resent always being the one to give in, it is probably best not to intervene. True, the other child may be taking advantage of the situation, but we are unlikely to accomplish much by stepping in. The best we can do is to work to reduce the demanding child's need to have things his way, helping him, at the same time, to develop greater tolerance toward frustration in general.

However, the child who gives in may resent it, and either come to us to complain about the situation or, worse, find ways to get back at the other youngster. In this case, parents ought to speak to him to help him with his problem. One can say to the child, "It is a wonderful character trait to be willing to forego. But you spoil it by feeling bad about it afterwards. It's nice to let others have their way, but you don't have to do it all the time. Make up your mind, before you give in, that you won't resent it afterwards, or else, it might be better not to give in to begin with."

## Peacemaking

While children usually manage to make peace between themselves after a fight, sometimes our peacemaking efforts are required. Judaism regards the pursuit of peace as an obligation: "Seek peace and pursue it."[19]

Aaron the priest had a peacemaking technique which we can use with our children. Whenever he heard that two people had had a quarrel, he would go to each one and tell him that the other was sorry and wanted to make up. Then when the two would meet again, they would hug one another and be friends.

Naturally, we must wait until the children have completely calmed down before trying this.

### HANDLING INSULTS

While children must know that insulting others is forbidden, they should be taught at the same time not to take it so seriously if anyone does it to them. Some children take offense very quickly, even when only mildly insulted or made fun of. We can ask the child, "How would you feel if someone said to you, 'Ha ha, you have three legs!' Would that hurt you? Of course not — because you wouldn't take it seriously. And if you didn't take it so seriously when someone makes fun of you, you wouldn't get into so many fights about it."

Children who easily get offended generally suffer from oversensitivity to negative judgment by others. One should help the child get over such oversensitivity by pointing out that just as it is not his business to judge others negatively, so is it no one else's business to judge him that way. If they do so anyway, it's their mistake, and he doesn't have to feel bad. He must be careful, though, not to judge others poorly for the way they judge him. In addition, one might tell a child that our sages view as real "heroes" those who are able to quietly bear insults. "Who suffer insults without repaying in kind; hear their shame and do not respond."[20]

One mother showed her children how the rain falls off her raincoat. Then she said to them, "You should be like my raincoat, and let all the unpleasant words fall off like rain."

## PROBLEM SOLVING AS A METHOD

In discussions with the children, we can bring up the problem of their fighting, eliciting their ideas on preventing fights. One mother reports a rather amusing but constructive talk with her two small children.

> I decided to call my two sons, Michael, age four, and Nathan, age five, for a little discussion about their frequent fighting. We had had such talks before on this and other subjects. Here is how our conversation went:
>
> Me: Look here Michael and Nathan, your fighting is becoming very unpleasant for all of us. Now do you have any good ideas as to how we could solve this problem?
>
> Michael: I think Nathan should move to a different house; he always bothers me and doesn't play nicely.
>
> Me: Well, that's not a good suggestion because Nathan belongs here — this is his family and Mommy and Daddy love him very much and will not have him living anywhere else.
>
> Nathan: (very serious) Well, maybe I'll just move

into the living room! I'll sleep on the couch and play here.

Me: That's not good because Mommy and Daddy use the living room at night and the lights will be on and there'll be noise. You won't be able to sleep.

Nathan: So maybe I'll just play here and sleep in my room. We don't fight at night — we sleep!

Both children thought this over for a moment while I just sat quietly. Then the discussion continued.

Michael: I think the best is just to try to be friends and get along 'cause I won't like playing by myself all the time.

Nathan: That will last exactly one half an hour.

Me: Well, let's see what we could do to make it last for more than half an hour. Let's discuss some of the problems.

Nathan: Michael insults me and says things that hurt my feelings.

Me: What could you do?

Nathan: I could ask him to stop but it won't help.

Me: Well, what do you think would happen if you just walked away?

Nathan: Good — I'll try that.

We continued to discuss different tactics which each could use when the trouble started.

Since this talk, I see a certain decrease in the fighting. I remind the kids of our discussion once in a while when things get a little out of hand, and it really helps.

At times you can explore with an individual child ways in which a fight could have been prevented. Tell him that we are not concerned with figuring out whose fault it was, but with finding ways to avoid fights in the future. For example, you can ask the child, after he has given you the details about a fight, "Let's think — what could you do next time when she ... ?" or "How could you say it next time so that ... ?" If the child can't think of anything, you can give suggestions.

In the following story, we see how a mother reviews two fights in which her son was involved, exploring with him ways to avoid such fights in the future.

My four-year-old Mosheh walked in from kindergarten and saw his sister, two and a half, writing with a ball pen on the table. He walked over and tried to grab the pen from her. She held onto it, and when he eventually succeeded in pulling it out of her hand, it drew a deep dark line from her forehead across her eye onto her cheek. She then hit him and a fight started between the two.

Later that day, Mosheh was building with some big plastic pieces on our living room carpet. The baby of nine months was nearby. Suddenly I heard a "clop" and loud crying. I ran in to see that he had thrown the baby behind the sofa, out of anger at him for taking one of the plastic pieces. I checked the baby and saw that he was, thank God, all right. Then I very firmly told my son that he must never do that again.

That night at bathtime, when Mosheh was relaxed and happy, I said to him, "I want to tell you a story. One day there was a big boy and he was building on the carpet and his little brother came over and took one of his pieces, and the boy took the baby brother and threw him down. The poor baby hurt himself really badly and was bleeding. He cried so so much. Thank God, after taking him to the doctor he was much better."

Then I said to him, "Mosheh, next time you're playing with your plastic pieces on the carpet and the baby comes over and takes a piece, what will you do?"

He answered, "I'll quickly pack up my plastic pieces and go to a high table."

"But what if you have already built something and you don't want to pack up? What will you do?"

"I'll take the baby to you and tell you he's bothering me."

"But if he keeps coming back?"

"I'll give him one or two pieces to play with, or maybe I'll start to build it inside my room and close the door."

"And what if your sister goes into the room and leaves the door open and the baby comes in and starts to take one of your pieces — what will you do then?"

"I'll carry the baby out of the room and close the door."

"You'll throw him outside the door?"

"Oh no — I'll put him gently down."

"How am I going to remind you to do this? I know that it's going to be hard to remember. Maybe I can say a word that will help you?"

"Say 'bedroom' or 'high table' and I'll remember."

"Now, assume you came home from kindergarten and you see your sister writing with a pen and paper at the table, and you want the pen. What do you do?"

"I'll ask her nicely, 'Please give me the pen.'"

"But suppose I had just given her the pen and she was about to write with it and she didn't want to give it to you. What will you do?"

"I'll come and ask you for another pen."

"And if I can't find or I don't have another pen — then what will you do?"

"I'll ask for a scissors."

We should not expect that our talks will have a sudden and dramatic impact. We need to be patient, demonstrating toward the child the very same tolerance we want him to develop toward others. We should show understanding with statements such as "I know how hard it is not to hit back when he punches you like that" or "I know it's difficult to take when she starts teasing you." If we need to rebuke the child for aggressive behavior, we should remember to do it gently.

It's a good idea to sum up, at the close of our discussion, "So, what are some of the things you're going to be working on?" In this way the child commits himself to work on self-improvement.

## The Child Who Hits Repeatedly

Sometimes a young child develops a habit of going over to other children and hitting them for no apparent reason. The parents are upset to see their child derive pleasure from such aggressive behavior. It can be especially painful for parents if the child acts this way in the presence of other adults, making them worry what the others are thinking not only about the child, but also about them.

Parents should make every effort to refrain from negative judgments such as "Why is he so mean to the other children!" These will only lead to angry criticism of the child. Rather, the behavior should be viewed as simply a bad habit. In addition to explaining to him that the Torah forbids us to hit, we should tell the child very quietly that he certainly wouldn't like it if others behaved this way toward him; thus he shouldn't do it to them.

The child needs to be handled with patience and understanding. Parents should keep in mind that it may not be so easy for him to give up his bad habit; this will help them ward off anger-producing thoughts such as "I've told him so many times not to hit — why does he continue to do it?" Parents should also worry less about what others are thinking about them because of the child's behavior, as such worrying often heightens their anger toward the child.

Occasionally, a teacher will report that a youngster is

hitting other children at school. Here is how one mother handled the situation:

My daughter of three, Channaleh, a clever and likable child, enjoyed hitting other children at her kindergarten for no apparent reason. She used to hit her brothers and sisters at home; when she started kindergarten, she began doing the same thing there. The teacher would put her into the corner as punishment, but this hadn't helped much. Since a new baby had arrived, the hitting at kindergarten had gotten much worse.

In a discussion of the problem during our weekly group meeting, I became aware that the child had learned to see herself exactly as I saw her. Questions such as "Why do you like to hit the other children?" had served only to reinforce this notion. It was as if a sign reading "I am a girl who likes to hit other children" had been pinned to her. I realized too that essentially, I had come to resign myself to the situation. As a result, so did my daughter. I did some thinking about the problem and the next day, had a good opportunity to try out my ideas.

I came to the kindergarten to pick up my daughter, and found her standing in the corner, looking very dejected. On our way home we had the following conversation:

"Why were you in the corner?"

"Because I hit Devorahle."

"Why did you hit her? Did she bother you — take something away from you?"

"No."

"Then why did you hit her?"

"Because I wanted her to cry."

"Do you like it when Devorahle cries?"

"Yes."

"And do you like to cry?"

"No."

"That's right, and I don't think Devorahle likes to cry either."

Now I asked her, "Why did God create us with hands? To hit others?" She said no. I asked, "Why do we have hands?" She answered, "To color, cut"; and I added, "And to help Mommy to pick up something which falls." Then I said, "You know, next time your hand wants to hit, tell it, 'Don't hit — come let's do something else.' And then quickly give it something else to do." At that point we arrived home.

The next morning I reminded her of our conversation of the day before. When I came to pick her up later from kindergarten, the teacher told me that she had not hit anyone once that day. I told her what I was doing to rid her of the habit, and suggested that she use the same method and that she stop putting her in the corner as punishment for hitting.

By the end of the following week, I learned from the teacher that my daughter had almost completely given up her former habit of hitting children.

Another mother used incentives to motivate her child to change his aggressive behavior at school.

Yehudah, three and a half, brought home a note from his rebbe (teacher) that he was hitting every day in school. I discussed it with the rebbe and asked him to send me a note each day to report on his behavior, and to remind Yehudah that for each good report his mother would give him a star. Ten stars would entitle him to a prize. I explained the arrangement to my son. Over a period of three weeks he improved rapidly to the point where the rebbe said that he never hit anymore.

When I visited the school afterwards, the children greeted me with a chorus of *"Yehudah lo marbitz!"* ("Yehudah doesn't hit!"). Whereas before he had been proud of his image as a "hitter," now he was equally proud of not hitting.

Sometimes, a child who hits at school can be kept home for a day.

 Crying

## The First Few Months

Crying is the baby's distress signal. It can communicate physical distress, such as hunger or indigestion, or emotional distress, such as displeasure over being left alone in the room. Although the average baby cries when he is hungry and, in addition, usually gets into at least one fretful period a day, there is wide variation in how much babies cry. Sometimes this is for purely physiological reasons: many babies, for instance, suffer from colic during the first three months after birth and will cry miserably for long spells. A different kind of determinant, however, can be far more crucial.

> Recent studies at the National Institute of Health show that, from birth onward, children exhibit clear-cut temperamental differences. When subjected in their cribs to such stimuli as cold discs, one child bawls vociferously while another calmly shifts an inch or two.[1]

Indeed, mothers themselves are often keenly aware of what seem to be innate personality traits in their babies — sometimes as early as during postnatal care in the hospital.

One newborn may seem fussy and irritable, while another is placid and easygoing; one is alert and sociable, while another is subdued and withdrawn, and so on.

This should be kept in mind when babies seem to cry excessively or for no reason. We are apt to fear that "something's wrong" when we've checked out everything — the baby is not sick, he's not hungry, he was properly burped, he's dry and comfortable — yet he continues to cry. Holding him may comfort him a bit, but he soon starts screaming as before. It is at this point that we have to guard against losing our self-confidence. The baby's crying makes a powerful demand on us to do something, and we are apt to feel inadequate when nothing we try seems to work. We may even feel personally rejected by the baby. Instead, we must assume that the baby is suffering from digestive pains and also, probably, from a rather low frustration tolerance. There is likely nothing we can do to make him stop crying altogether.

Mothers should not let themselves become frantic over a baby's crying and start nervously asking "What's the matter? Why are you crying?"; this is likely to make the baby cry even more. Instead, the mother should try to keep herself calm by reminding herself that, while highly unpleasant and irritating, the crying is *not* unbearable.

There are, of course, some measures we can take that may at least reduce the baby's crying. For instance, a pacifier can often help calm the baby. Some mothers hold their baby whenever he cries, speaking to him in a soothing and comforting voice; others will at times permit him to "cry it out" alone. There is no correct way here and every mother can decide what is best for her.

In the meantime, the mother need not suffer unnecessarily. When she feels the need for some respite, she can close the door to the baby's room and listen to music. She should not feel guilty over doing this; after all, she cannot function as an effective mother if she is worn-out from her baby's crying. Of course, she should check up frequently on the baby to make sure he's all right. It is also advisable to have a baby-sitter come in and relieve her for a few hours once or twice a week, enabling her to get away from the house.

## SPOILING

There is little danger of spoiling the baby during the first two or three months. Parents can feel free to hold the baby when he is miserable without fearing that he will come to demand this all the time. The fact that the baby stops crying as soon as we pick him up and walk him around does not necessarily mean he is spoiled. More likely, the comfort of being held distracts him momentarily from his pains.

As the baby grows older, we should be more careful. If we now continue to pick him up and rock him or walk him around every time he cries, he could well become accustomed to such service. It can be difficult to ignore our little one's wails, but it may sometimes be better for ourselves and the baby if we harden our hearts a bit and let him cry. By now we have probably learned to differentiate between types of crying that have to be responded to and types that can be safely ignored. Obviously, if we have been holding the baby and he begins to cry as soon as we put him down, we know that all he wants is to be held. Here we must control our compassion. The child has to learn to accept that we cannot hold him all the time. We can talk to him soothingly, explaining that we are sorry he is so miserable but we can't hold him right now. He won't understand our words, but our gentle voice will comfort him and help him to accept reality.

## Beyond Six Months: Nighttime Crying

By the age of six months, most babies no longer need to be fed at night. Many babies even give up the nighttime feeding on their own well before this time.

Others, however, continue to cry at night. A mother who

does not mind getting up might decide to continue to give the night feeding. But many mothers find that the nighttime interruptions interfere with their functioning. For them, it will be necessary to train the baby to sleep through. Usually this can be done only by allowing him to "cry it out." On the first night the baby is apt to cry for an hour or so, but on succeeding nights the crying quickly tapers off. This method can be used successfully even with older babies who have not yet been trained to sleep through the night.

One mother had been giving her baby a nighttime bottle for over a year simply because she felt she did not have the energy to train him to do without it. When she finally decided that enough was enough, she found that it was much less trouble than she had imagined. The first night he cried for fifty minutes, the second night for thirty; by the fourth night he was down to only ten minutes. The fifth night he woke up, whimpered a bit, but when he saw that it didn't help, went right back to sleep. Within the week the crying had completely stopped.

It is good to keep the door to the baby's room slightly ajar, and position his crib so that we can peek in on him without his noticing us. This way we can check to make sure there isn't some serious reason for his crying, such as a hand or foot caught in the crib bars.

A baby who has been sleeping well through the night for some time may suddenly start waking up again. This often happens after a bad cold when the baby has gotten used to having the parents at his bedside. The same treatment can be used. It usually takes no more than two or three nights for the baby to learn that he gains nothing from his crying.

If other children who sleep in the same room complain about being woken up, we can explain to them why the baby is being allowed to cry. It may not be so easy with neighbors who come to complain about the noise. A heavy blanket draped over the window will absorb the sound to some extent, as will a thick rug on the floor. We can also try to explain to the neighbors that the crying is likely to last for only a few nights.

Occasionally, a particularly highstrung and sensitive baby will keep up the nighttime crying well past the age when other babies give it up, often screaming for hours at a time. The parents become worn-out and exhausted from sleepless nights; all efforts to break him of his habit fail. Health problems such as allergies and recurrent sickness often predispose a child to such crying. It can sometimes help to go in for a few minutes, talk soothingly to the child expressing empathy for his discomfort, and then put him gently down. There may, however, be no one solution to this problem. It's good to keep in mind that these children eventually settle down to a normal sleeping pattern.


## As the Child Grows Older

As long as a child is not yet able to talk, he will continue to let us know when he wants something mainly by crying. This is a difficult stage. We must try to be patient and to avoid asking the child in irritation "What do you want?" or offering him various things to make him stop. If it proves impossible — as is sometimes the case — to find out what the child wants, we should stop trying and just speak to him soothingly. The crying may be unpleasant, but if we remain calm the child is more likely to get over his frustration and eventually quiet down.

By meeting his demands while he is still unable to talk, we inevitably reinforce crying behavior in the child. We can, however, minimize it — by, for example, taking the child out of his playpen before he becomes too unhappy in it; this way we won't end up having to do it by the time he is screaming. The same goes for the high chair. If a child always gets into crying spells when he is overtired, don't wait with putting him to bed until he reaches that state, but do it at the first sign of crankiness.

## DEALING WITH CRYING

*Empathic responses.* As long as our children are still small, we must be prepared to tolerate a certain amount of crying. Parents should work on reacting, not with annoyance, but with calmness and empathy. It will help them to do so if they remind themselves that showing irritation will only make the child feel worse and cry more. They should also keep in mind that by reacting calmly to the child's crying, they provide him a model of how to cope better with *his* frustrations.

When your child is crying because you refused him some wish, don't tell him "It won't help you to cry — you're not getting it"; rather, say to him quietly, "I'm sorry, but I can't give you what you want." Sometimes a crying child is trying to tell us something, but is so upset that it is impossible to understand him. If we tell him "Stop crying — I can't understand a word you're saying," it comes across as uncaring. An empathic response such as "I'd like to listen to you, but I can't understand you when you're crying" generally has a calming effect on the child.

Likewise, it is better not to ask, when a child comes running to us in tears, "What are you crying about?" Rather, we should say, with obvious concern, "What happened, honey?" Avoid especially remarks such as "Come on, it's enough. Stop crying already."

Children often scream and carry on about some minor mishap, like a torn book. Here too remarks such as "Come on, that's nothing to cry over" are unlikely to be well received by the child. Usually, it is best to show mild sympathy and then allow the child to get over his distress by himself. At times, we might try helping the child to see things in a better perspective. For example, we might say to him, "I can see you're upset about the book, but this kind of crying should be saved for when something really bad happens."

A child's crying after hurting himself should always be related to with empathy. Impatient to get the child to stop his crying, parents will often make light of bangs or minor cuts and bruises, saying "Come on, nothing happened, it's just a little scratch" or "Stop crying, you didn't hurt yourself all that much." They will find that this usually makes the child cry harder and longer. On the other hand, a sympathetic "Oh, you fell! Where did you hurt yourself?" or "That must really hurt you!" is far more likely to quiet him. If there are visible marks, we should examine these seriously as we say, "Come, let's put something on it and it'll make it better." Some ointment, vaseline, or even powder will do.

*Problem solving.* Children can often be diverted from crying if we help them adopt a problem-solving orientation. A good way to do this is to say to the child, "Let's look for a solution." Once he is busy thinking of solutions, he usually forgets about crying.

*Humor.* Gentle humor can sometimes distract a child from crying. For example, when the child cries because his toy has just broken or fallen apart, we can examine it very seriously as we say, "Hmm — maybe we'd better call the building company and have them send an engineer to put this together again," and then smile. Or, we might say, as we examine some minor scratch or bruise, "Hmm — let me see — how many kisses do you think you need for this? Will five be enough?" Few children will be able to repress a smile in response to this.

## COMMON TYPES OF CRYING

*Nighttime fears.* Small children frequently go through a period of waking up at night frightened. The child may have had a nightmare, or simply be afraid of the dark. A few soothing words, with reassurance that we are there to protect him, will usually calm him down. If the child is afraid of some shadowy object in his room which he imagines to be an animal or "bad man," we should gently show him that his fears are groundless.

One mother describes how she calmed her young child:

> My daughter Malkah woke up crying one night. I went in and found her wide-eyed and terrified. I asked her why she was frightened and she said, "There's a bird in my room." I asked, "Where is the bird?" She pointed in the direction of her little-kiddie car and said, "Over there. That's the bird." There was enough light in the room to see clearly, so I picked up the car and asked, "This is the bird? No, this is a kiddie-car, not a bird." She took a few moments and then smiled, saying, "I thought the kiddie-car was a bird!" Then I told her she must now go to sleep. "Everything is okay," I said, "Daddy's in his bed, the baby is in his bed, you and your sister are in your beds. I'm going to my bed too, and I'm still looking after you. Everything is okay." Satisfied that she was all right, I kissed her and went out of the room.

A child who wakes up frightened at night will often come crying into his parents' room. Although it may be a great temptation for one of the parents to take the child into the bed, this usually turns out to be a mistake. Once the child has gotten used to coming into a parent's bed, it is no easy job getting him out again. It is better not to let him in to begin with, but to bring him back to his own bed and calm him there.

*Crying when mother leaves.* Young children often cry when their mother leaves the house. Although they usually stop two or three minutes after she has gone, some mothers feel terribly guilty about leaving a crying child. They cannot bear to see their child so miserable and think themselves heartless to go out and leave him this way. The child, in turn, often senses his mother's hesitation and guilt and learns to play on it, intensifying his crying so as to keep the mother home.

Once she understands what causes her guilt, the mother will be able to challenge the validity of her thoughts and, as a result, begin to feel more comfortable about leaving the house. The child, too, will find it easier to accept his mother's absence.

My two-year-old son Eli was a real Mommy's boy, meaning, he wanted to be near me at all times. This became a big problem when I had to go out and leave him with a baby-sitter or at someone else's house. When I did leave him, which was seldom, I would act apologetic and console him; but I would still hear his screams from quite a distance. When I would return, I would hear that he'd screamed a lot, almost the whole time. This made me feel very guilty about leaving him, and I therefore tried not to have to do it. I only went out when it was absolutely necessary. If I had to go out, I felt so insecure about it. "How will he manage? How can I do this to him? I shouldn't leave him in such a state! Am I a bad mother if I leave my child screaming?"

Through discussing it in the group, I began to identify these thoughts as the ones that were causing my guilt. I realized what my mistake was: the assumption that Eli was being harmed by my leaving. This, of course, was not really true. He was capable of learning to tolerate the fact that I was going away. It was okay for me to go out.

As I got used to thinking this way, I felt more secure about leaving him. The next time I wanted to go out, I just told him that I had to in a matter-of-fact way. He cried much less. Now, he cries for no longer than two or three minutes at the most.

*Resistant crying.* A balky two-year-old will sometimes resist his mother's efforts to get him to do what she wants with vehement screaming. One can avoid getting into head-on confrontations by firmly taking the child's hand and leading him through his various routines, basically ignoring his carrying on. For instance, if the youngster is screaming because he does not want to leave the house with us, we pull him along, all the while talking to him in a soothing voice: "I know, you don't want to go — but we're going anyway. Okay — everything's all right." We should continue talking to the child about other things; this distracts him and helps him forget his distress.

At times, one firm spank will do the trick. It should be given soon after the child begins acting up and with conviction, as we say to him, "Okay, that's enough now." It is a mistake to postpone the spanking until we are worn-out from the child's screaming, for we are then likely to give it in anger.

*Temper tantrums.* Temper tantrums are common in young children, and are nothing to worry about. Tantrums are an expression of the young child's outrage at having been thwarted in some way. Although they generally occur more often in children who have low frustration tolerance, parents should keep in mind that their reactions can play an important role in helping to minimize this tendency.

Parents need to experiment to see what approach works best with their child. A bit of comfort and some gentle words at the onset of a tantrum can often quickly calm the child down. As this mother's experience shows:

> My baby of a year and a half would work himself into fierce crying fits whenever we didn't give him what he wanted. At first I handled the situation by ignoring him completely. I was very consistent, but it didn't help. Next I tried being firm with him by picking him up, putting him in his bed, and telling him that he had to stay there until he stopped. That helped a bit, but he still continued doing it. Then I tried comforting him. I held him and spoke to him soothingly: "I'm sorry — I know you really wanted (such and such) but I can't give it to you. It's not worth making yourself sick over it." We did this consistently and after three days, he stopped it completely.

With older children, it is usually best to take no notice, except for a sympathetic "I'm sorry, but I can't let you have what you want." Let the child thrash about on the floor while you go about your business as usual. The child will stop on his own when he sees that the tantrum gets him nowhere.

Sometimes the best way to handle tantrums is to lead the child to his room as we say, "I see you're having a tantrum. Come, I'll take you to your room and you can have the tantrum there." The child sometimes just needs to be by himself for a while, as this mother discovered:

> My son Aaron was in the midst of having a tantrum. I told him to please remain in his room until he felt he could restrain himself. I peeked into his room and found him under his crib. All of a sudden he gave a loud screech. Then there was silence. Two minutes later he emerged from his room and announced, "Mommy, I'm all finished now."

More alarming than simple thrashing about in a fit of temper are head banging and breath holding spells. If the child is furiously banging his head so that you fear real damage to the brain, you must of course stop him. Hold the child firmly, as you talk to him soothingly. Remember to keep calm yourself; this is reassuring to the child and helps him over his temper fit.

> Whenever something didn't go her way, my three-year-old would bang her head on the floor or furniture until she was black and blue. Afraid of giving in and spoiling her, I would let her do it; but I felt physically ill watching her. Now that I was advised to hold her and calm her instead, I felt that a weight had been lifted from my chest!
>
> I had always been very nervous about denying her things because of her head banging. When she would come to demand some snack food, I would give

in to her more than I felt I should. And so she could end up eating most of the morning. Now I felt more confident. I began responding by stroking her cheek and quietly saying no. If she stamped her foot, I'd quietly hold the foot down.

In the past, when I tried to put her to bed for naptime, she would frequently fuss or scream, and I would immediately take her out. Now I softly stroke her cheek, quietly saying, "It's time for a nap now. Put your head down," and she quietly lies down. Within two weeks she's a different child.

In breath holding, the child, who is extremely frustrated and has been crying furiously, suddenly begins to hold his breath so that the oxygen supply to the brain is cut off and the child turns blue (or sometimes white). He may lose consciousness momentarily, or go into convulsions similar to those in epileptic fits. All this is, of course, very alarming to the parents.

A well-known pediatrician[2] with much experience in the treatment of breath holding advises that parents should not try to prevent their child's breath holding by keeping him from all crying fits. This makes parents very apprehensive and apt to give in to everything. Parents must also be very careful not to show alarm at breath holding, for if they do, the child will use these spells more and more to get his way. Instead, as soon as he begins to hold his breath, the parents should go out of the room and leave the child alone. Nothing will happen to him; if he faints, his muscles immediately relax so that breathing starts again immediately. In fact, when the child sees that he has no audience, his breath often returns to him quickly and he does not reach the fainting or convulsion stage. The parents can keep an eye on the child through a slightly open door so that, in case he faints, they can go in and lay him down on his side. After the child has calmed down, the parents should make sure to show him some warmth and affection.

Parents should always consult with an experienced

pediatrician for a proper diagnosis and to rule out epilepsy or other illness. It is helpful to know that children usually outgrow this problem as they get older.

*Whining and clinging.* Young children are more apt to be cranky and whiny when they are tired. When you suspect tiredness as the reason for a child's unpleasant behavior, it's best to lead him quietly to his bed as you say, "Come — you're tired. Lie down a bit."

Children who have just recuperated from some illness may also whine a lot, clinging constantly to the mother and demanding the same extra attention they received while they were sick. We have to be prepared to put up with a week or so of crankiness, offering the child comfort while we accustom him to a more normal state of affairs.

Whining and clinging behavior can be very irritating, and parents have to make special efforts to refrain from outbursts such as "Stop your whining already — it's getting on my nerves!" or "I can't stand your clinging to me all the time!" When a child has gotten used to saying everything in a whining voice, telling him calmly "Talk, don't whine" can be an effective way of ridding him of this unpleasant habit. Or, when a child whines, "Mo-o-mmy I'm thirrrsty, I wanna dri-ink," try telling him gently, "You know, when you talk that way it doesn't sound so nice. Suppose you say that again now, in another voice — like this: 'Mommy I'm thirsty — can I have a drink?'" Now you can tell the child when he whines, "Can you say that again with your *other* voice?" followed by "See, it sounds so much better when you talk."

Clinging behavior can be discouraged by telling the child softly, "Honey, I can't work when you cling to me this way" or "It doesn't feel so nice to have my dress pulled at." It may also help to bring in some toys and let the child play near you on the floor.

We don't, of course, always have to listen to a child's prolonged whining and crying. We can tell the child, "I see you're miserable and I'm very sorry about it. But the whining hurts my ears. I'm going to turn the radio on to hear a little music, so the noise won't bother me so much." (A "walkman"-type tape recorder is excellent for this.) Or, the child can be pleasantly asked to go to his room until he is finished with his whining.

Parents sometimes unwittingly reinforce the child's whining behavior. For example, a mother takes her child out for a walk in the stroller. When the mother stops to chat with a friend, the child starts to squirm and whine; the mother says to her friend, "She doesn't like it when I stop to talk to anyone." This is like giving the child a license to continue acting that way. Instead, it's best to quietly tell him, "We'll be going again right away. Mommy is just talking to her friend for a minute." Of course, don't try the child's patience by talking interminably with a friend while the child is strapped in his stroller. Let the child out, if he can walk, or keep the conversation short.

# 13 The School: Assisting in the Educational Endeavor

Until the Talmudic period, Jewish children were educated exclusively by their parents. The child was taught Torah and some trade or craft by which to earn a living at home. Because of a danger that Torah might be forgotten, Yehoshua ben Gamla established, at the beginning of the Talmudic period, an innovation of major importance — the world's first system of public education.[1] Whereas before parents bore the sole responsibility for teaching their children, they could now delegate some of this responsibility to others. It must be kept in mind, however, that in the area of moral training, the school can only assist parents in their work. Here, the parents' job remains primary. The home is the ideal environment for molding the child's character.

## Assuming a Supportive Role

In choosing a school, we will make extensive inquiries in order to find the best possible learning environment for our child. Once a decision has been made, we must entrust the child to the school's care and assume a supportive role. Naturally, a school is only as good as its teachers, and teachers, sadly, are not always the perfect examples we would like for our children. Often they are far from the prescribed ideal: "If the teacher is like an angel of God, they shall seek Torah from his mouth; if not, they shall not seek Torah from his mouth."[2] Still, we must try to be tolerant, difficult though it can sometimes be. However dissatisfied we may be, we must never talk about it in front of our children, as this is likely to foster disrespect for their school and teachers.

In addition to giving the school their full support, parents should regularly visit their child's teacher to discuss the child's progress and find out about any special problems.

## Misbehavior at School

Parents naturally measure their success by their children's behavior. This is why, when they hear that their child misbehaves at school, they see it as a sign of their failure. Knowing that others, too, see them as having failed increases the pain.

Parents' reactions vary. Some get angry at the child and punish him for bringing such shame upon them. Others get angry at the teacher, blaming him for the problem. Neither approach is constructive.

To be able to deal effectively with the situation, we have to begin by identifying the true sources of our anger — our sense of failure and our feelings of shame — and deal with these. When we evaluate ourselves negatively because of our child's poor conduct, it is because we are assuming that it must be our fault. But the child's misbehavior at school could be due to other reasons. Remember that even if parents were to do everything right (if that were indeed possible!), it still would not guarantee them perfectly behaved children. In any case, it is best not to be involved with global evaluation of ourselves, nor with the concomitant worry about what others think of us.

Once we are feeling calm, we should talk to the child and let him tell his side of the story. We might say gently, "You know, I heard some unpleasant things about you from the teacher. Could you tell me what's happening?" Whatever problems the child raises, we should relate to them seriously. Perhaps some of these can be solved by some tactful intervention on our part. But no matter what difficulties he is having, the child must know that he has to respect his teachers, especially his Torah teacher.[3]

Often the misbehaving child is only trying to have fun. In this case he needs a serious talk about how his behavior creates difficulties for the teacher. An incentive system, with the child earning points for good reports which he brings home from school, can sometimes motivate him to improve his behavior. While punishment can be tried in serious cases, it is usually better to leave disciplinary actions to the school.

While we must not immediately blame the teacher for the child's faulty conduct, we do have to keep in mind that poor teaching skills or poor control of the class are often at the bottom of the problem. However, the child should never see himself as in the right. Certainly, as already mentioned, he must never hear us berate the school or belittle the teacher.

## Handling Complaints About the Teacher

When children come with complaints about their teacher, don't get involved in a discussion over who was right or wrong. Hear the child out first, keeping in mind that we are not permitted to accept what he tells us as the absolute truth. After you have listened to the child's story, ask him, "Are you telling me this because you think I can help you in some way? Then I want to know about it. But if you're telling it to me because you're mad at the teacher and you want me to know how bad he is, then it's *leshon hara*' and you're not allowed to tell it to me."

We have to help the child realize that anger always comes from judging others negatively, and teach him to judge his teacher's actions favorably. At the same time, we can help the child to be more accepting of the situation by showing empathy.  We might say, for example, "I'm so sorry you're having a hard time, but you're not allowed to tell me *leshon hara'* about the teacher." Even if we have sound reasons to believe that the teacher was at fault, we can still say, "Maybe the teacher made a mistake, but . . ."

Parents should encourage their child to talk over any problems with the teacher himself. He can ask to talk to him during recess. If the child hesitates because he is afraid the teacher will regard this as *chutzpah*, you can rehearse with him what he will say, making sure it will be said respectfully.

## Learning Difficulties

Many educators today still believe that children do not enjoy learning, that when left to do as they please they would prefer to play, and that they must, therefore, be stimulated to study by grades and other competitive methods.  To realize how untrue this notion is, one has only to visit a Montessori kindergarten and observe children of three and four at work without any incentive from without.  (One mother took her children out of such a kindergarten because, as she put it, "All they wanted to do when they came home was wash the walls and windows!")  Maria Montessori, the Italian founder of this system of education, maintained that children feel a great need to do constructive work: "It is certain that the child's aptitude for work represents a vital instinct."[4]  Apparently, when God blessed the newly created first couple with the commandment to "fill the earth and conquer it," He implanted in them a drive to control and shape their environment, a drive which can already be seen in young children.

The saying "The jealousy of *sofrim* increases knowledge" is frequently quoted to justify the use of competition. However, the word *sofrim* refers here to teachers and not students. The correct interpretation of this saying, which is merely an observation on human nature and in no way a recommendation, is that jealousy among teachers causes them to become better educators.[5]

The grading system, thought by so many as necessary to stimulate students to better achievement, actually causes much harm. It creates in the child's mind a false association between accomplishment and esteem. Objectively viewed, a grade on a test or report card is nothing more than a rating of a child's knowledge in a particular subject. However, teachers generally convey to their pupils a quite different meaning. A high grade is something to be proud of; it shows that the child has paid attention and studied well; thus he is a "good" student and worthy of esteem. A low grade, on the other hand, is something to be ashamed of; it indicates that the child has not applied himself sufficiently; he is therefore a poor or "bad" student and consequently held in low esteem. That success in learning depends as much on intellectual ability as on diligence seems to have been entirely overlooked.

Unfortunately, this attitude is frequently carried over into the home. Parents express pride and satisfaction in the child who is a good student, but show disappointment and displeasure toward the child who does badly at school. This goes contrary to the Jewish approach, which values the individual not according to his intellectual achievement, but according to his righteousness. This is only as it should be, for God has seen fit to endow us with different levels of intellectual ability. Only in respect to righteousness do we have equal opportunities, since righteousness is defined in terms of our individual potential. "Every person has the ability to be as righteous as our teacher, Mosheh,"[6] although surely not as wise.

There are, of course, youngsters who do poorly in school not because they lack ability but because they lack self-discipline; we should keep in mind also that some children are unable to achieve because of a learning disability (see below). All too often, however, the poor student is a child of mediocre intellectual ability who, though he tries hard, can't really do any better. In most cases, unfortunately, no recognition is taken of this. Both parents and teachers urge the child to make greater effort. The child, who does try harder but still fails to do much better, inevitably concludes that it is his fault and that he must somehow be inferior. In such a situation the child naturally loses much of his motivation for learning, and is unlikely to continue exerting himself for long. It then, in turn, becomes easy to point to the child's lack of effort as the reason for his poor performance.

But even the good student may be harmed by a competitive system. Some successful students develop such a strong need to be held in high esteem that they strive excessively to excel, and are dissatisfied unless they are always on top. Such perfectionism often makes children tense and anxious about their studies; see the discussion below.

The ideal solution to these achievement problems would be a learning system that permitted each child to advance at his own pace, and in which grades, if used at all, would be given for achievement *relative* to the child's ability.*

> The teacher can help each child set his own standards of performance for what he would learn and reward *every* child for making progress toward his particular goals. A test is merely a way to find out what the child has learned so he can be rewarded for it and a way to diagnose what difficulties the child may have so he knows what he has yet to learn.[7]

Interestingly, in the old time cheder the practice was for the rebbe (teacher) to test each child separately. Written tests and report cards, as we know them today, were unheard of. In addition, the Jewish approach to education has always stressed the need for individualization in education: "Teach the lad according to his nature."[8] The Talmud contains the

---

* High school marks which serve as a basis for admission to institutions of higher learning must, of course, be based on absolute standards.

story of Rav Preida, who had a student with whom he had to repeat the lesson 400 times.[9] Maharsha views this not merely as an example of unusual patience and devotion, but as the fulfillment of an *obligation* for all teachers to teach the lesson over and over until the student knows it thoroughly.[10] Moreover, we find in the Shulchan 'Arukh: "A teacher must not become angry with his pupils if they do not understand him, but must repeat his explanation as many times as necessary until they understand."[11]

Today, parents will have a hard time finding schools that live up to these ideals. In the meantime, they can foster in their children a serious attitude toward their studies without, however, setting up high standards of accomplishment. For instance, they should not tell a child who got an 85 on a test, "You could have done better." In general, it is best to praise children for diligence rather than for high marks. They should be encouraged to study in order to acquire knowledge, and not in order to get praise or recognition.

When a child with mediocre learning ability shows unhappiness over his low grades, we can tell him, "To us it doesn't matter what marks you get. The main thing is that you're doing your best." We should also emphasize that the merit achieved through Torah study is not measured in terms of our success, but in terms of the sincerity of our effort.[12] The more effort we make, the greater the reward.[13]

## THE UNDERACHIEVER

The underachiever is a child with good intellectual ability who lacks the self-discipline to apply himself to his studies. He hates the school regimen and, though forced to sit in the classroom, usually absorbs little instruction there. Teachers find it frustrating to have such a child in their class; here is a potentially capable youngster just frittering his time away.

While parents may worry over what will become of their child, there is actually less reason for concern than one might think. After wasting most of their elementary school years, these children generally start buckling down to their studies later in high school. As long as the child has acquired basic skills such as reading and arithmetic, he can easily make up for the lost years since most of the material he missed earlier will be reviewed.

In the meantime, the best thing parents can do is to commiserate with their child about his dislike for school, while at the same time encouraging him to apply himself more seriously. The message to the child should be, "I know how much you hate school, but since you have to be there anyway, why not try to learn something." Critical remarks about low marks should be avoided. Instead, parents should note any improvements, no matter how small, and comment on these. For example: "I notice you're doing better in Chumash — you went up from a D to a C."

## THE CHILD WITH A LEARNING DISABILITY

Learning disabilities can range from mild to severe. Here we will focus only on the milder form; with the severe form, special education will usually be required.

To most parents, it comes as a shock to hear that their child has a learning disability. Typically, nothing is noticed until the child enters first grade. There, he does not learn to read as do the other children. Often the child has difficulty in writing and arithmetic as well. Fortunately, most schools today have special programs for these children called "main-streaming," in which they must leave their regular class for only an hour or so a day of specialized educational therapy.

Learning disability must not be confused with mental slowness. In mental retardation, the child functions poorly because of an inherently limited intellectual capacity. The typical learning disabled child, on the other hand, has normal or even above average intelligence; his problems stem from a perceptual handicap.

Learning disability must also not be confused with so-called developmental lag. The child cannot be kept another year in kindergarten with the expectation that he will "outgrow" his problem; he must receive specialized educational help with a trained teacher. With early detection and treatment, there is every hope that the child will eventually overcome his original disability completely.

The child with a learning disability needs strong support from his parents at home. His problem should be talked about openly and frankly, with the other siblings informed of it as well. If any siblings ridicule the child for asking inappropriate or naive questions, or show lack of understanding of the child's problems in other ways, they should be reminded of his disability and helped to develop a more sympathetic attitude.

## THE STRIVING AND TENSE CHILD

This child can do well but, because he believes that a person must achieve outstandingly in order to have worth, pushes himself to the point where he becomes tense and nervous. Before an exam he worries incessantly; afterwards he upbraids himself over every wrong answer, wondering "How could I make such a stupid mistake?" Parents often unwittingly contribute to the child's problem by telling him, even when he has done reasonably well, that he should have done better. If he sees that he cannot maintain the standards of perfection he has set for himself, the child, while of good intelligence, may even give up and become an intellectual "dropout" from school.

To these children, too, parents must stress that a person is rated according to his righteousness, not intellectual achievement, and that striving for excellence is commendable as long as the goal is not acclaim or recognition. The parents should show pleasure over the fact that their child enjoys learning, rather than praising him for his high marks.

211

## Homework

Homework should be seen as the child's responsibility. Parents should remain in the background, giving support and perhaps some minor assistance now and then; they should never let homework become a daily affair of reminders, unpleasant nagging, or even threatening and scolding.

For homework to have meaning, it must be graded to the child's capacity so that he can work independently with little assistance from us. If their child's assignments are too difficult for him, parents should ask the teacher to adjust the work accordingly.

When we notice that a child is negligent about doing his homework, we should have a quiet talk with him in which we convey our concern, explaining the importance of doing his school assignments. However, we will not remind him about homework since it is his responsibility. We might ask the child to decide on a convenient time for doing the homework, but we should then stay out of the picture. If the teacher complains about the child's negligence, we can say that we are very sorry about it, but while we encourage our children to do their assignments we prefer not to let it become an issue at home. This leaves it up to the teacher to deal with the problem.

Certainly it is desirable that children do their homework. But parents should ask themselves whether it is worth their while to be engaged in daily battle over it, making everyone miserable and spoiling the home environment.

# 14 Common Problems

## Eating

In his book on baby and child care, Dr. Benjamin Spock writes:

> Why do so many children eat poorly? Most commonly because so many mothers are conscientious about trying to make them eat well. You don't see many feeding problems in puppies, or among young humans in places where mothers don't know enough about diet to worry. You might say jokingly that it takes knowledge and many months of hard work to make a feeding problem.
>
> One child seems to be born with a wolf's appetite that stays big even when he's unhappy or sick. Another's appetite is more moderate and is easily affected by his health and spirits. The first child seems to be cut out to be plump; the second is apparently intended to stay on the slender side. But *every* baby is born with enough appetite to keep him healthy, keep him gaining at the proper rate for him.[1]

Parents can spare themselves much unnecessary misery over feeding problems by following one basic rule: Don't urge and certainly never force a child to eat. Children have a natural and inborn desire for food. When they are hungry enough they will eat.

A mother might hesitate to put this advice into practice for fear that if she allows her child to eat just what he pleases, he may develop some nutritional deficiency. Dr. Spock notes that there is rarely any such danger.

> It's important to remember that children have a remarkable inborn mechanism that lets them know how much food and which types of food they need for normal growth and development. It is extremely rare to see serious malnutrition or vitamin deficiency or infectious disease result from a feeding problem.[2]

Dr. Spock describes Dr. Clara Davis's well-known experiments in appetite. Babies of eight to ten months were allowed to choose their own diet from a variety of wholesome unrefined foods. The babies developed very well over a period of time, choosing what any scientist would agree was a well-balanced diet.

Nevertheless, parents of a child who is eating poorly are advised to have a doctor check him from time to time, to evaluate the diet he is taking for what it provides and what it lacks, and recommend substitute foods or medical preparations if necessary.

## AVOIDING FEEDING PROBLEMS

We should start from the very beginning to show confidence in children's inborn capacity to judge what is good for them. Don't try to make a baby finish more of his bottle than he wants. Introduce solids gradually; when a baby refuses some food, take it away. You can try offering it again after a few weeks. If the baby's appetite goes down for a while and he seems to want to eat very little (sometimes due to teething), make no effort to get him to eat more. Children should come to think of food as something they want, not as a favor they do us.

Mothers often make the mistake of continuing to feed a baby when it is obvious that he has lost interest in his food. When an infant begins to fool around or turns his head away from the spoon, assume he's had enough; take him out of his highchair and end the meal.

Or there may be one particular food — usually some vegetable — which the baby dislikes. The mother insists on his taking it anyway, trying by hook or by crook to get it down him. Sometimes she will even try mixing it with some other food which the child likes. Usually, however, children are not so easily fooled. Even if the child eats the food, he may notice something strange about its taste and start to become suspicious of foods in general. Parents should ask themselves: Is it worth it? After all, many adults, too, have a food or two that they just don't like. The child's aversion is probably very real, and we cause him real suffering (and ourselves much trouble) every time we put him through this ordeal.

As they grow older, children's tastes and appetites will continue to vary, resulting at times in balkiness about eating. This can easily develop into a feeding problem. The worried mother urges the child to eat more — but the child eats even less. The mother's anxiety may turn into anger, as she begins to feel increasingly frustrated by the child's refusal to eat; this, however, only serves to further reduce his appetite. Mealtimes become scenes of conflict and wrangling. The child not only comes to view eating as something he does to please his mother, he often starts seeing himself as bad for not eating as his parents want him to.

To avoid these problems, parents must make a determined effort to stop worrying so much about their child's food intake, and rely on his natural appetite to establish a pattern that is right for him. Keep in mind that there are no "good" or "bad" eaters; only children with big or small appetites. Don't measure your success by how much your child eats. Once anxiety is gone, parents will be less likely to become upset over their child's poor eating habits.

Neither is it necessary to battle with children who have trouble finishing what's on their plate. We can avoid the entire problem by simply allowing the child to help himself, or by asking him how much he wants first and giving him *only* what he specifies. (In fact, it is best in general to give very small servings so that the child has to ask for more.) With the child thus in control of what is on his plate, we should not have to insist too hard that he finish. If he still doesn't want to eat the food, we should tell him, "Okay, I guess you're not hungry now; you can eat it later." (Warm food should be reheated for palatability.) Children should be taught that it is wrong to throw away food.[3]

## THE FUSSY EATER

Some children's problems with eating go beyond a vegetable or two; the fussy eater refuses to touch a wide range of foods. Parents should try their best to be tolerant and to refrain from comments about his fussiness. Don't coax him or try to make him eat "just a little bit"; don't offer him something special if he eats; don't threaten to deprive him of his dessert. If there is nothing he likes at a particular meal, he can always have bread with butter or margarine. (Five slices of bread contain nine grams of protein!)

Some parents believe a child should learn to eat everything. Certainly this is desirable; the question is how to accomplish it. Fussy children are serious about their dislikes, and if we try to simply force them to eat something we are going to have a fight on our hands.

We can always, from time to time, suggest that a child try something he has until now rejected. We might explain that our taste frequently changes and, if we give ourselves a chance, we often discover that we like something we thought we'd never eat.

We do not, however, have to go out of our way to cater to such children. While parents should be considerate and try to include in the menu foods which the child likes, they should certainly not prepare special foods just for him. A firm policy here will also help the child to eventually eat more foods.

If a child hasn't eaten at mealtime, be sure not to let him fill up afterwards on "junk" food or even on fruit. The child should be told beforehand that no food (beyond a regular snack) is served between meals; this way he knows what to expect if he chooses not to eat. This must not be said in a threatening manner, such as "If you don't eat now, you're not getting anything else until supper." The child should be allowed to have crackers or fruit with everyone else at snacktime.

A mother may feel terribly guilty at the idea of letting a child go hungry. After all, it is her responsibility to provide him with food; isn't she a bad mother if she sees her child go hungry and does nothing about it? She should realize, however, that it was the child's choice not to eat. The small amount of hunger which he may feel (we should not forget that he vastly exaggerates this hunger to get us to pity him!) will do him no harm; it will teach him to eat when everyone else does — at mealtimes. We can sympathize with the child when he complains of being hungry, but, for his good, we stick to our decision.

Fussy children often express dislike for a particular food by saying "Yich!" or "I hate this!" Although a child may say that he does not care for something, he should never show disgust for food as this demonstrates lack of respect for what God provides. If he does not want to eat something that is being served, he can say "No, thank you" or "I'd rather not have any."

## ILLNESS

A child generally has a poor appetite while he is sick. Even after he recovers, it may take a while until he begins to eat normally again. Feeding problems often begin here when an anxious parent starts to push food on the child prematurely.

Parents should offer the child only the drinks and solids he wants, and wait patiently until his appetite returns to normal. There is no need to worry about weight loss; when the child's appetite comes back he is usually ravenously hungry and quickly gains back whatever may have been lost.

## THE THIN CHILD; THE OVERWEIGHT CHILD

Thinness is usually a matter of constitution. However, if parents are worried, they should consult the child's doctor to rule out any medical reasons for the child's thinness.

Dr. Spock's opinion is that as long as the child doesn't seem to show any special problem, has been slender since infancy but gains a reasonable amount of weight every year, parents can relax and let him alone. No doubt the child was meant to be that way.

As for overweight, an important factor behind it is heredity. A child's chances of being overweight are highest if both parents tend to plumpness, less if only one of the parents has this tendency. If the propensity exists, the only way to combat it is to regulate the child's food intake. If we begin while the child is yet young to accustom him to eating non-calorie rich foods, it can greatly minimize his chances of being overweight. This means refraining from serving fatty foods or rich desserts. Instead of cookies, pretzels, and the like, snacks can consist of fresh fruit or carrot and cucumber sticks.

Parents should keep in mind that well-fed often means overfed. There is no reason to worry about a little "baby fat"; however, if an older baby looks as if he is getting heavy, it would be wise to cut down somewhat on starchy foods and concentrate more on fruits and vegetables.

If your child is fat, encourage him to be sensible about what he eats. Don't, however, tell him things like "You're too fat — you shouldn't eat so much bread." Also, don't keep the child from eating the rich foods served for special occasions, such as Shabbath; he will certainly feel enormously deprived and it may even increase his craving for those foods.

Some children don't seem the least bit troubled by their excess fat. Others, however, are very unhappy about it. These children are usually very critical of themselves for eating too much, blaming themselves for their poor self-control. The typical pattern of the overweight person is to tell himself as he reaches for some calorie-rich food, "I really shouldn't eat this, but . . ."; afterwards, he reprimands himself. To help the child, get him to understand this cycle and teach him first to stop telling himself off for indulging. He should realize how difficult dieting is and that it takes tremendous will power to lose weight. Parents should sympathize with the child over his difficulties in losing weight and certainly not add to his misery by calling attention to how he looks.

It usually doesn't help to push a child to lose weight. However, older children, in particular adolescents, can often be persuaded to consult with a doctor who can, if necessary, prescribe a suitable diet.

## Lying

We must distinguish between the young child's tendency to confuse fantasy and reality, and deliberate lying. The former is common among children with lively imaginations. Rather than expressing disbelief, it is better to respond with mild amazement. For instance, if a four-year-old tells us "I saw a lion on the street!" we might simply answer, "Really!"

Deliberate distortions of truth are another matter. Most children will on occasion resort to lying to avoid scoldings or punishments, or to evade responsibilities. Some children will also conjure up stories about themselves to gain acclaim and recognition.

When we suspect that a child is not telling the truth, we have to be careful not to accuse him of it right away. It is best to gently confront him; if he insists he is telling the truth, give him the benefit of the doubt.

However, if we are certain that the child is lying, we must have a quiet talk with him about it. We should tell him that we know he is not telling the truth and then explain that lying is forbidden.[4] In addition, we should impress upon him how important it is that we be able to rely on what he tells us.

Nevertheless, while the child has to know that he is forbidden to lie, we should not frighten him about it. Keep in mind that even though a child knows lying is wrong, he may at times resort to it anyway. If too big an issue has been made over lying, he might then feel terribly guilty.

When a child denies having done something in order to avoid being reprimanded or punished, assure him that you will do neither. It is more important that the child be encouraged to tell the truth. Afterwards you can say, "I'm glad you told me the truth. Please, never be afraid to admit it when you did something wrong." Naturally, we have to be careful in general that our reprimands for misdeeds be mild, so that the child will not be frightened into lying.

Much defensive lying can be prevented by steering clear of the kinds of questions that so often provoke it. For example, if we notice that our child has run off right after finishing the meal, we should not ask him "Did you say *birkhath hamazon*?" (grace after meals) but say instead, "You'd better come back to the table — you forgot to say *birkhath hamazon*."

When their child lies a great deal, parents naturally worry that he will become a confirmed liar. There is usually no reason for such anxiety. Though children do sometimes go through a phase of persistent lying, with proper handling they gradually give it up. The important thing is to react calmly and continue to impress upon the child how important it is for him to always tell the truth so that others can rely on him.

## Stealing

Young children often lack a clear sense of what belongs to them and what doesn't. When they want to take home an attractive toy from the store or a playmate's house, we should not call it stealing. All we need do is explain to the child that the toy does not belong to him, gently persuading him to give it up. Likewise, when he helps himself to candy in the supermarket we tell him that it belongs to the store and make him put it back on the shelf. By the time they are six, children are capable of understanding what stealing is and that it is wrong.

When parents first learn that their child has carried out a more serious theft, they usually react with alarm. Stealing, after all, is a crime and it is frightening to associate their child with it. After getting over their initial shock the parents may look for motives. They may even blame themselves: "Where have *we* gone wrong that he needs to steal?"

Seeking psychological explanations for the child's behavior is usually not helpful. The most simple and logical reason for stealing is that the child badly wants something which does not belong to him and, though he knows it is wrong, takes it anyway or steals money in order to buy it. Neither is it constructive for parents to try to figure out where they have failed. Instead, they should focus on the problem itself and what to do about it.

To begin with, we must make sure that the child understands that stealing is a serious transgression.[5] One mother who discovered that her five year old was taking money from her purse reacted by reprimanding him sharply; yet the child continued taking money. She then had a serious talk with him, explaining that stealing is not allowed. This made a strong impression on the child and he stopped taking money.

It is also important, if you are sure your child has stolen something, to confront him directly. For instance, you notice that a twenty-dollar bill is missing from your purse. That same day your son comes home and shows you a brand new watch which he claims to have found on the street. Don't ask, "Are you sure you found it?" Tell him, "Twenty dollars is missing from my wallet. You took that money and bought the watch with it." If the child denies having taken the money, don't get drawn into an argument, but quietly persist. When he does finally admit the theft, make him return the watch and give you back the money. (If the stolen money was spent on candy or other treats, we must discuss with the child ways to reimburse whomever the money was stolen from.)

A child who has stolen something should never be shamed or called a thief; nor should he be frightened with visions of ending up in jail one day. Also, don't ask him "Why did you do it?" as this is only likely to set off self-denigrating thought patterns.

Even if we are careful to avoid these mistakes, children who steal will often still feel enormously guilty about it afterwards. In helping the child to cope with these feelings, we should try first to get him to talk about them. We might start by asking, "You feel very bad about what you did, don't you?" The child may hang his head and say nothing; usually, this is a sign that he feels too ashamed to answer. We should continue nevertheless, by gently reminding him that even though he did something very bad, it does not make *him* a bad person. Rather, than thinking how terrible he is, he should just be sorry and make up his mind not to do something like this again. Then he can be sure that God will forgive him. We can also advise the child to come and talk to us from now on, whenever there is something he wants badly.

## Bad Language

Children use bad language chiefly because of the enormous reaction it gets from shocked grown-ups. Frequently they have no idea what the words mean; all they know is that by saying them, they have the power to scandalize everyone around them.

It is important to avoid these shocked reactions. The first time your child uses unfit language, let him know quietly that these are not nice words and that you don't want him to use them. Your reaction should be very low-keyed. If he does it again, tell him calmly, "I asked you not to use that word." The child might also be told "These are garbage words — they don't belong in your mouth." For older children a mild rebuke such as "I don't expect you to talk that way" can be helpful. They should be taught also, that obscene language (*nivul peh*) debases both speaker and listener and is condemned by the Torah in the strongest terms.[6]

This does not mean that you must react each time the child uses bad language. If you have the impression that your remarks are encouraging him to keep it up, it may be best to ignore the child for a while. Whichever way you choose to handle it, the main thing is to stay calm.

## Wild Behavior

All children tend occasionally to get out of control. They start running around the house, over and under the furniture, in and out, sometimes tumbling over each other, screaming most of the time at the top of their lungs. For the kids, it's great fun; but not for the grown-ups, whom it usually leaves feeling exhausted and at their wit's end.

It's best to call the children to one room, saying that you have something important to tell them. Once they are together, say, "Kids, I know you're having a lot of fun, but I can't let you run around like this here. It's okay for outside but not in the house. Now, if you can play quietly, fine. If not, I'll have to put you into separate rooms. You decide, okay?" If this does not help, tell them, "All right kids, into separate rooms — you can come out when you're ready to play quietly," and lead each one to a different room.

Some mothers hesitate to stop their children from making noise, telling themselves, "Kids have to run around and let out energy, and I shouldn't let it bother me so much. I should be able to tolerate it." They would do better to be less demanding of themselves; why let our nerves take a needless beating? In the end it's bound to come out in yelling at the children. Other mothers feel badly about breaking up their children's fun. Interestingly, one sometimes gets the impression when watching kids running wild that they've had enough, but have gotten into a state where they cannot stop themselves. In other words, we might actually be doing them a kindness by stopping them.

## Shyness

Shyness, when not exaggerated, is actually a positive character trait. It is one of the three outstanding qualities which characterize the Jewish people.[7]

Some children seem to be born with a tendency toward shyness. In contrast to the outgoing youngster who has a ready grin for any stranger, the shy child is apt to draw away from a visitor's friendly overtures. Parents should not, out of embarrassment over the child's behavior, chide "Why are you so shy?" or "Someone talked to you — why don't you answer?" Nor, however, should they excuse him with, for instance, "He's always like that with visitors," as this will most likely only reinforce the shyness. Moreover, by calling attention to the child's shyness in this way, we make him come to see it as something bad.

Parents must try not to be concerned about the impression their child makes. While they should encourage the child to be friendly, they should not make an issue of it if he fails to respond to someone's "Hello" or "How are you." When a visitor thoughtlessly remarks "My, isn't she shy" they can answer, "No, she's not shy. She'll talk in a little while, when she's gotten used to you." Even the normally outgoing youngster may at times feel overwhelmed by a grown-up's overly enthusiastic show of friendliness, especially when he is being bombarded with questions which he does not at the moment feel like answering.

The less said about a child's shyness, the better. As they grow older, these children generally lose much of their shyness and become more sociable.

# Notes

## INTRODUCTION

1. *Midrash Mishleh* 31:10.
2. The parents' obligation to educate their children has several aspects. Their obligation to accustom them to fulfilling the mitzvoth is a Rabbinic commandment (*Sukkah* 42 a, *Chagigah* 4a) and the father's obligation to teach his son Torah is a divine command (Deuteronomy 11:19). In addition, the father is obliged to teach his son good character traits and a trade (cf. Rambam, Commentary on the Mishnah, *Makoth* 2:3). See also Rabbi Samson Raphael Hirsch, *Horeb*, Vol. 2, trans. by Dayan Dr. I. Grunfeld (London: Soncino Press, 1975), sec. 548.
3. *Even Shelemah* 6:5.
4. Rabbi Samson Raphael Hirsch, *Yesodoth Hachinukh*, Vol. 2, trans. by A. Wolf (Bnei Brak: Netzach Publishers, 1968), p. 54.
5. *Sefer Hachinukh* 16.

## CHAPTER 1

1. Walen, DiGuiseppe, and Wessler, *A Practitioner's Guide to Rational Emotive Therapy* (New York: Oxford University Press, 1980).
2. *Sotah* 3b, and Rashi there.
3. *Nedarim* 22a.
4. *Pesachim* 113b.
5. *Shabbath* 105b.
6. Loc. cit.; see Rambam, Mishneh Torah, Hil. De'oth 2:3.
7. Personal communication.
8. Carol Tavris, *Anger: The Misunderstood Emotion* (New York: Simon & Schuster, 1983).
9. See Chapter 2, Notes 33, 34.
10. Leviticus 25:17; *Bava Metzi'a* 58b; Shulchan 'Arukh, Choshen Mishpat 228.
11. *Sefer Hachinukh* 338.
12. *Shabbath* 105b.
13. *Avoth* 2:4.
14. Rambam, op. cit., Hil. Teshuvah 3:2.
15. *Avoth* 1:6.
16. Rabbi Samson Raphael Hirsch, *Horeb*, Vol. 1, trans. by Dayan Dr. I. Grunfeld, (London: Soncino Press, 1975), Sec. 138.
17. Cited in Rabbi Zelig Pliskin, *Love Your Neighbor* (Jerusalem: Aish HaTorah Publications, 1977), pp. 287-288.
18. Ecclesiastes 7:20.
19. *Avoth* 2:16.
20. Rambam, op. cit., 7:3.
21. See Rambam, op. cit., 6.
22. Jeremiah 31:18.
23. *Der Israelit* (8 IX 36).
24. Dov Katz *Tenu'ath Hamusar*, Vol. 1, p. 284.

# Notes

25. *Avoth* 2:13.
26. Rambam, Commentary on the Mishnah, *Avoth* 2:13.
27. Rabbenu Yonah, commentary, *Avoth* 2:13.
28. *Avoth* 3:14.
29. Mishnah *Sanhedrin* 4:5.
30. All but the most severe transgressions (those entailing *kareth* — "cutting off," or worse) are forgiven upon *teshuvah* and the passing of Yom Kippur (*Yoma* 86a).
31. *Yoma* 86b and *Iyun Ya'akov* in *Eyn Ya'akov*, there.
32. This seems to be implied by the verse cited there (". . . like a fool reciting his foolishness," Proverbs 26:11).
33. The two sides of this issue appear to be the subject of a Talmudic debate (*Yoma* 86b). However, Rif and Rosh accept both sides as relevant, implying that they are reconcilable. The above paragraph is an attempt at such reconciliation.
34. Mishnah *Yoma* 8:9; Rambam, Mishneh Torah, Hil. Teshuvah 2:9.
35. Rudolf Dreikurs, *The Challenge of Parenthood* (New York: Duell, Sloan & Pearce, 1948), p. 96.
36. Rabbi Samson Raphael Hirsch, op. cit., Vol. 2, Sec. 519.

## CHAPTER 2

1. *Menorath Hamaor* 163, referring to *Kiddushin* 30b.
2. *Kiddushin* 30b.
3. *Sefer Hachinukh* 33.
4. Rabbi Yaakov Kamenicki, personal communication.
5. Shulchan 'Arukh, *Yoreh De'ah* 240:19.
6. Cited in Rabbi Meir E. H. Munk, *S'khar Veha'anasha Bechinukh* (Bnei Brak: Hamesorah, 1982), p. 38.
7. Exodus 20:12.
8. Leviticus 19:3.
9. *Kiddushin* 31b.
10. Mishnah *Kiddushin* 1:7.
11. Shulchan 'Arukh *Yoreh De'ah* 240:14.
12. Mishnah *Kerithoth* 6:9. Though in principle the honor due the mother is equal that due the father, in practice, if both parents have asked for the child's help, the father is to be given precedence because the mother, too, is required to honor him. When this obligation falls away due to a divorce, the child may assign precedence according to his own judgment.
13. Rambam, Commentary on the Mishnah, *Kiddushin* 1:7.
14. Rabbi Eliezer of Metz, *Sefer Yere-im*, sec. 56 (in R. Y. I. Goldblum's edition, sec. 221-2); R. Menahem HaMe'iri, *Beth HaBechira, Kiddushin* 31a (in R. A. Sofer's edition p. 181).
15. *'Arukh Hashulchan, Yoreh De'ah* 240:8.
16. *Sefer Haredim* 1:26.
17. Shulchan 'Arukh, *Yoreh De'ah* 240:2.
18. Chazon Ish, *Yoreh De'ah*, 149.

19. Rabbi Yoel Schwartz, *Beth Abba* (Jerusalem: Jerusalem Academy of Jewish Studies, 1978), p. 91.
20. Shulchan 'Arukh, *Yoreh De'ah* 240:2.
21. Loc. cit.
22. *Pischai Teshuvah* Ibid. 240:2.
23. *Igroth Moshe, Yoreh De'ah* Vol. 1, sec. 133 (p. 272).
24. *Chayey Adam* 67:11.
25. Deuteronomy 27:16.
26. Rambam, Mishneh Torah, Hil. Mamrim 5:15.
27. *Sheiltoth* 60; *Ha'amek Sheela* there, no. 6.
28. *Chayey Adam* 67:3.
29. Rambam, op. cit., 6:3.
30. Rabbi Yerucham F. Perlow, commentary to *Sefer Hamitzvoth* of Rabbi Sa'adiah Gaon, Com. 9, s.v. *ume'atah nomar.*
31. *Bereishith Rabbah* 65:16.
32. *Sefer Hamiknah* on *Kiddushin* 31b.
33. *Teshuvoth Rabbi Akiva Eger*, Pesakim 68.
34. Loc. cit. Indeed, it appears that this question is subject to a dispute among early authorities. For an extensive discussion, see above, Note 31, s.v. *ela sheraithi.* Rabbi Perlow concludes there (s.v. *we-amnam afilu*) that obedience is included in the mitzvah of reverence.
35. Personal communication.
36. *Avoth* 4:12.
37. Rabbi Samson Raphael Hirsch, *Yesodoth Hachinukh*, Vol. 1, trans. by A. Wolf and S. Pushinsky (Bnei Brak: Netzach Publishers, 1968), pp. 66-67.
38. Rabbi S. R. Hirsch, op. cit., Vol. 2, trans. by A. Wolf, pp. 54, 57.

## CHAPTER 3

1. Cf. Rambam, Commentary on the Mishnah, *Makoth* 2:3.
2. J. and H. Krumboltz, *Changing Children's Behavior* (New Jersey: Prentice-Hall, 1972), p. 243.
3. *Midrash Rabbah, Koheleth* 1:13, s.v. *venathati eth libi.*
4. *Koheleth* 5:9.
5. James Dobson, *Dare to Discipline* (New York: Bantam Books, 1970), p. 31.
6. Rabbi Samson Raphael Hirsch, *Yesodoth Hachinukh*, Vol. 2, trans. by A. Wolf (Bnei Brak: Netzach Publishers, 1968), p. 54.
7. See Introduction, Note 2.
8. Rabbi S. R. Hirsch, *Judaism Eternal*, Vol. 1, trans. by Dayan Dr. I. Grunfeld (London: Soncino Press, 1956), p. 230.

## CHAPTER 4

1. Cited in Rabbi Zelig Pliskin, *Love Your Neighbor* (Jerusalem: Aish HaTorah Publications, 1977), p. 374.
2. *Shemoth Rabbah* 20:10.
3. *Mekhilta Shemoth* 19:5.

# Notes

4. *Avoth* 2:8.
5. *Avoth* 2:16.
6. *Sotah* 22b.
7. *Avoth* 1:3.
8. *Ta'anith* 24a.
9. Rambam, Commentary to the Mishnah, *Sanhedrin*, Chapter 10, Introduction.
10. Rabbi Yoel Schwartz, *The Eternal Jewish Home* (Jerusalem: Jerusalem Academy of Jewish Studies, 1982), pp. 78-79.

## CHAPTER 5

1. Proverbs 3:12.
2. Proverbs 13:24.
3. Rabbi Shlomoh Wolbe, *Aley Shur* (Be-er Yaakov: 1972), p. 261.
4. Proverbs 29:17.
5. Job 11:12.
6. *Sotah* 47a.
7. Rabbi Samson Raphael Hirsch, *Yesodoth Hachinukh,* Vol. 1, trans. by A. Wolf and S. Pushinsky (Bnei Brak: Netzach Publishers, 1968), pp. 65, 66.
8. *Midrash Rabbah,* Exodus, beginning.
9. James Dobson, *Dare to Discipline* (New York: Bantam Books, 1970), pp. 2-3.
10. Leviticus 19:17.
11. Rambam, Mishneh Torah, Hil. Teshuvah 4:1; *Shulchan 'Arukh Harav,* Talmud Torah 1:6.
12. Rambam, op. cit., Hil. De'oth 6:7.
13. *Yevamoth* 65b.
14. *Lev Eliyahu,* Vol. 2, pp. 26-27.
15. Rambam, op. cit., 6:7 and 8.
16. *Semag* prohibition 6 and *Brith Mosheh* there.
17. *Shabbath* 105b. See also Rambam, op. cit., 2:3.
18. *Avoth deRabbi Nathan* 12:3.
19. *Derashoth HaRan,* No. 9, beginning.
20. Cited in Rabbi Yoel Schwartz, *The Eternal Jewish Home* (Jerusalem: Jerusalem Academy of Jewish Studies, 1982), p. 63.
21. Haim G. Ginott, *Teacher and Child* (New York: Avon Books, 1975), p. 83.
22. Rabbi Samson Raphael Hirsch, op. cit., p. 69.
23. *Even Shelemah* 6:5.
24. "Even though he learns, it is a mitzvah [to hit him]" (*Makoth* 8a), presumably only when it is necessary for his character development. This is implied by the verse cited there (Note 4 above). For confirmation of this interpretation, compare Rambam, Commentary on the Mishnah, *Makoth* 2:3).
25. Rabbi Shlomoh Wolbe, op. cit., p. 260.
26. Ibid., p. 261.

27. "[God] never punishes without previous warning" (*Sanhedrin* 56b) and we are to emulate God's ways (Deuteronomy 13:5; *Sotah* 14a).
28. *Semachoth* 2:6.
29. *Reshith Chokhmah*, P. Gidul Habanim, s.v. *vetzarikh ha-adam.*
30. *Sanhedrin* 85a from Deuteronomy 25:3; Shulchan 'Arukh, Choshen Mishpat 420:1.
31. *Shulchan 'Arukh Harav*, Choshen Mishpat, Hil. Nizkey Guf Vanefesh 4.
32. Rabbi Samson Raphael Hirsch, op. cit., Vol. 2, trans. by A. Wolf, p. 65.
33. *Bava Bathra* 21a.
34. *Even Shelemah* 6:4.
35. Shulchan 'Arukh, *Yoreh De'ah* 240:20.
36. Numbers 19:14.
37. Rabbi Akiva Eger on *Yoreh De'ah* 240:20.

## CHAPTER 6

1. Leviticus 19:18.
2. Rambam, Mishneh Torah, Hil. Evel 14:1.
3. Rabbi Shlomoh Wolbe, *Aley Shur* (Be-er Yaakov: 1972), p. 93.
4. *Yerushalmi Nedarim* 9:4. See also Psalms 89:3.

## CHAPTER 7

1. Leviticus 25:17.
2. *Avoth* 1:2.
3. Tosefta *Pe-ah* 4, 18-19.
4. Mikhah 6:8.
5. Rabbi Yisrael Meir Kagan (Chafetz Chaim), *Ahavath Chesed*, part 2, Chs. 1 and 2.
6. *Bava Metzi'a* 58b.
7. "That which is hateful to you, do not do to your fellow. This is the entire Torah; the rest is commentary" (*Shabbath* 31a).
8. Psalms 89:3; *Avoth* 1:2.
9. Rabbi Eliyahu E. Dessler, *Mikhtav MeEliyahu* Vol. 1, ed. by Rabbi Aryeh Carmel, Rabbi Alter Halpern, pp. 34-35.
10. *Sefer Hachinukh* 16.
11. Rudolf Dreikurs, *The Challenge of Parenthood* (New York: Duell, Sloan & Pearce, 1948), p. 156.
12. *Avoth de Rabbi Nathan* 11. See also Yehudah Levi, *Shaarey Talmud Torah* (Jerusalem: Feldheim, 1981), pp. 195-199.
13. Netziv, *Ha'amek Davar*, Genesis 2:4.
14. *Avoth* 1:10.
15. Rabbi Yoel Schwartz, *The Eternal Jewish Home* (Jerusalem: Jerusalem Academy of Jewish Studies, 1982), p. 78.
16. Isaiah 58:7; *Tana DeBey Eliyahu Rabbah* 27, begin.; Shulchan 'Arukh, *Yoreh De'ah* 251:3.

17. *Shabbath* 31a.
18. *Yoma* 86a.
19. *Berakhoth* 6b. Under certain circumstances, one should even interrupt the reading of the *Shema'* to greet a person (Mishnah *Berakhoth* 2:1).
20. *Avoth* 5:7.
21. *Chagigah* 5a.

## CHAPTER 8

1. *Sefer Hachinukh* 16. See also *Mesilath Yesharim* 7.
2. *Gittin* 67a; Rashi, s.v. *otzar balum.*
3. *Sanhedrin* 86a.
4. Cited in Rabbi Yoel Schwartz, *The Eternal Jewish Home* (Jerusalem: Jerusalem Academy of Jewish Studies, 1982), p. 80.
5. *Avodah Zarah* 20b and Maharsha there.
6. *Shabbath* 50b; *Vayikra Rabbah* 34:3.
7. *Berakhoth* 53b, based on Leviticus 11:44.

## CHAPTER 10

1. *Shabbath* 10b.

## CHAPTER 11

1. Psalms 133:1.
2. *Sanhedrin* 58b; Shulchan 'Arukh, Choshen Mishpat 420:1.
3. Shulchan 'Arukh, Choshen Mishpat 421:13; *Shulchan 'Arukh Harav*, Choshen Mishpat, Hilkhoth Nizkey Guf Vanefesh 2. See also Note 11, below.
4. Ibid., 4.
5. Leviticus 25:17; Shulchan 'Arukh, Choshen Mishpat 228:1.
6. Loc. cit.; *Bava Metzi'a* 58b; Rambam, Mishneh Torah, Hil. De'oth 6:8 & Hil. Teshuvah 3:14.
7. Maharshal to Semag (Neg. 6).
8. Rabbi Yisrael Meir Kagan, *Chafetz Chaim* 4:10-11.
9. Ibid., 8:11.
10. *Pesachim* 118a, based on Exodus 23:1.
11. Leviticus 19:18. From a passage in *Yoma* 23a it appears that one may bear a grudge over a physical attack or an insult, until the apology is received. However, revenge is never permitted. See also Rambam, op. cit., Hil. De'oth 7:7: "... in all matters of the world." Other authorities permit even revenge for physical or verbal attacks. We have based the text on the conclusion of Rabbi Y.M. Kagan (*Chafetz Chayim*, Introduction, Note 8-9), who discusses the issue at length.
12. *Avoth* 1:6 and *Shavuoth* 30a.
13. Rambam, op. cit., 6:6-7.
14. *Avoth* 2:4.

15. Leviticus 19:17; Rambam, op. cit. 6:6-7.
16. *Yevamoth* 65b. Brought by Rosh, there.
17. Mishnah *Yoma* 8:9; Rambam, op. cit., Hil. Teshuvah 2:9.
18. *Avoth* 4:1.
19. Psalms 34:15.
20. *Shabbath* 88b.

## CHAPTER 12

1. Cited in Albert Ellis, *How to Raise An Emotionally Healthy Child* (California: Wilshire Book Co., 1978), p. 5.
2. Dr. Uri Levi, Poria, Israel.

## CHAPTER 13

1. *Bava Bathra* 21a.
2. *Moed Katan* 17a.
3. *Yoreh De'ah* 242:1.
4. Maria Montessori, *The Secret of Childhood* (New York: Frederick A. Stokes, 1939), p. 208.
5. *Baba Bathra* 21a.
6. Rambam, Mishneh Torah, Hil. Teshuvah 5:2.
7. J. and H. Krumboltz, *Changing Children's Behavior* (New Jersey: Prentice-Hall, 1972), p. 195.
8. Proverbs 22:6.
9. *Eiruvin* 54b.
10. *Chidushey Agadah, Sanhedrin* 91b, s.v. *kol hamone'a*.
11. Shulchan 'Arukh, *Yoreh De'ah* 246:10.
12. "The one who accomplishes more is equal to the one who accomplishes less, as long as his intention is to do the will of Heaven" (*Berakhoth* 5b).
13. *Avoth* 5:22.

## CHAPTER 14

1. Benjamin Spock, *The Common Sense Book of Baby and Child Care* (New York: Duell, Sloan & Pearce, 1962), pp. 423-424.
2. Ibid., p. 426.
3. *Shabbath* 129a; Rambam, Mishneh Torah, Hil. Melakhim 6:10.
4. Exodus 23:7; *Sotah* 42a.
5. Leviticus 19:11.
6. Isaiah 9:16; *Shabbath* 33a.
7. *Yevamoth* 79a.

# Index

# Index

# Index